August 2008

For Nick --

Blessings And Peace!

Shae Stanford
1 Cor. 15:58

When God Disappears is truly one of the most candid and sincere exposés of trusting God and living life even when we are overwhelmed by struggles, challenges, and those unexpected curve balls that life sometimes throws at us. This very timely piece has been carefully written, and is sure to transcend denominational, ethnic and social echelons.

Vivian Berryhill
President and Founder
National Coalition of Pastors' Spouses

In the tradition of sensitive poets, struggling saints and wise sages, Shane Stanford takes us on an honest and hopeful journey into the hard and barren places of our lives. There, amid our cry of absence, we confront a Presence who shares the burdens, opens a new future and joins our journey toward wholeness. *When God Disappears* is a refreshing spring of living water in a dry and thirsty land!

Bishop Kenneth L. Carder
Ruth W. and A. Morris Williams, Jr., Professor of the Practice of Christian Ministry
Duke Divinity School

Shane Stanford has delightfully illumined the intersection of real life and faith with very real stories of very real people encountering a very real God. Well done! I am still pondering in my heart Mary, Sophie and Carol. Their stories will resonate in my soul for years to come.

Allen Hunt
Host, *The Allen Hunt Show*

My first encounters with Jesus came in the form of His loving followers. His presence continues to be most visible, as Shane shares in these six encounters, through people who love like Jesus, touch like Jesus, care like Jesus *and become Jesus to the marginalized and hurting.*

Mike Slaughter
Lead Pastor, Ginghamsburg UMC, Tipp City, Ohio

I was prepared for *When God Disappears* to be a beautifully written book, and it is. I wasn't prepared for the way it reached into the depths of my soul and brought to the surface hurts that I had neatly tucked away, and then exposed those hurts to the light of Jesus' healing love and forgiveness. This is a life-changing book!

Dr. Bev Smallwood
Psychologist and author of *This Wasn't Supposed to Happen to Me: 10 Make-or-Break Choices When Life Steals Your Dreams and Rocks Your World*

By the second chapter of *When God Disappears*, my reading a book had turned into living a story—a story that I shall continue to live for the rest of my life. Stanford's story gives us astonishingly powerful grammar from which we can conjugate life's losses, sorrows and despairs as well as joys and hopes.

Dr. Leonard Sweet
Drew Theological School, George Fox University
www.sermons.com

Shane Stanford points us to God's radiant piercing of *miseri*. He teaches us to recognize divine presence in divine absence, to celebrate the living light of God, and to cherish one another along the way. As we show up and engage our spiritual journeys with Shane, we become braver, more honest, more deeply faithful.

Bishop Hope Morgan Ward
Episcopal Leader, Mississippi Annual Conference of the United Methodist Church

While boldly engaging the difficulty and complexity of this world's pain and suffering, Stanford illumines the message of God's steadfast love with and for those in the most desperate of life's situations. With remarkable insight and candor, Stanford offers a refreshing glimpse into God's love for those who have lost their grasp on hope through personal and biblical narrative. This book is truly a gem!

Dr. Laceye Warner
Associate Dean for Academics, Duke University Divinity School

A few years ago, I was intrigued by the title *The Seven Next Words of Christ*. I quickly devoured it! I loved the book, but even more importantly, I loved the author. I discovered that Shane Stanford and I share a passion for hurting people, and over the years, he has become a trusted friend and brother.

Kay Warren
Executive Director, HIV/AIDS Initiative, Saddleback Church

Shane Stanford writes with power and conviction about real life with all its joys and imperfections. He tells the stories of ordinary and extraordinary people in a captivating way that permits the faith he proclaims to come alive. *When God Disappears* is a rare book that you will immediately want to share with the most dedicated Christian you know as well as those struggling with faith.

Dr. Lovett H. Weems, Jr.
Distinguished Professor of Church Leadership
Wesley Theological Seminary, Washington, DC

FINDING HOPE WHEN
YOUR CIRCUMSTANCES
SEEM IMPOSSIBLE

WHEN

GOD

DISAPPEARS

Shane Stanford

SHANE STANFORD

Regal

From Gospel Light
Ventura, California, U.S.A.

Published by Regal
From Gospel Light
Ventura, California, U.S.A.
www.regalbooks.com
Printed in the U.S.A.

Library of Congress Cataloging-in-Publication Data
Stanford, Shane, 1970-
When God disappears : finding hope when your circumstances seem impossible /
Shane Stanford.
p. cm.
ISBN 978-0-8307-4660-6 (hard cover) — 978-0-8307-4800-6
(international trade paper)
1. Hidden God. 2. Consolation. 3. Hope—Religious aspects—Christianity. I. Title.
BT180.H54S73 2008
248.8'6—dc22
2008018807

1 2 3 4 5 6 7 8 9 10 / 15 14 13 12 11 10 09 08

Rights for publishing this book outside the U.S.A. or in non-English languages are
administered by Gospel Light Worldwide, an international not-for-profit ministry.
For additional information, please visit www.glww.org, email info@glww.org, or write
to Gospel Light Worldwide, 1957 Eastman Avenue, Ventura, CA 93003, U.S.A.

For Pokey—
The bridge is strong.
I love you.

So, my dear brothers and sisters,

be strong and steady, always enthusiastic

about the Lord's work, for you know that

nothing you do for the Lord

is ever useless.

1 CORINTHIANS 15:58

Contents

When God Disappears is an amazing book that will, no doubt, touch the lives of all its readers. It teaches of God's love and patience for us, and it represents one of the most unique reading experiences I have ever encountered. It will give you the hope you have so desperately been searching to find.

Shane Stanford's life is an example for all of us who long for meaning in our lives. Living with hemophilia, Hepatitis-C and HIV, one might expect to find repression and discrimination, rejection by family and friends and fear of the unknown, yet Shane has sustained an unwavering faith. Many people would have turned away from God, would have given up hope and lost faith. Yet he continues to see God's grace and to teach others about a loving God who never gives up on His children.

Without a doubt, there are times in the lives of every individual when the giants seem too big, the trees too high to climb and the rocks plentiful for those who throw them. We have all experienced times of rejection, pain, loss, failure and sorrow. Yet, as Shane demonstrates, these are the times that can deepen our faith.

The sting of death has touched us all. It casts a lonely darkness that can only be illuminated by the hand of God. Shane reminds us that it is our faith and trust in God that soothes our wounded spirits in these painful moments of life. His words walk us gently to the foot of the cross, where acceptance always lives, death and illness cannot exist, trust is never lost, promises are never broken and everyone is always welcome.

We have all been guilty of betrayal at some point in our lives. How are we to react when someone betrays us? When someone chooses to momentarily look away from our friendship and deceive us? Shane shows us that forgiveness is the only path to restoration.

Many times, we forget to include God in our lives and decision-making. We only turn to God during the trying times, the times when we are going through trials and tribulations. When things are great in our lives, however, we often forget to praise God and include Him in our decisions. It's only later that we discover decisions made without His help lead to remorse. God must be in our lives daily, not just during the trying times.

I am so grateful that Shane has allowed me to be a part of his journey. I pray that you, too, will be ministered to and touched by his amazing words. It is my hope that you will choose to live a life in honor of our Lord and Savior, Jesus Christ. He is truly amazing!

Deanna Favre
Founder, Deanna Favre Hope Foundation
New York Times Bestselling Author, *Don't Bet Against Me*
Wife of NFL Quarterback Brett Favre
Hattiesburg, Mississippi

ACKNOWLEDGMENTS

Of all the pages I write, these are always the most difficult. How do you say "thank you" to everyone who has helped such a project come to life? As it is impossible to name each person who has influenced the words of this book, I trust that anyone not singled out here knows who they are and how much they mean to me.

In particular, I am grateful to the following:

To Chip MacGregor, a committed and faithful agent, whose skill brought this project to life.

To Steven Lawson, Kim Bangs, Aly Hawkins, Mark Weising, Rob Williams and everyone at Regal, for believing that my words could make a difference.

To Jeane Wynn, for her tireless efforts in making sure the message is heard far and wide.

To the staff and Board of Directors of *The United Methodist Hour*, for your unending support and patience. You "make a difference" . . .

To Chris, for your pastoral care, encouragement and guidance.

To Laurie and Jill, for your assistance and support in keeping me organized and sane.

To Robbie, Nagen, Joe and Teresa, for making sure my body was as willing as my mind and spirit.

To Anthony, for your friendship and partnership in the weekly, great adventure of God's grace.

To the Group—the Kents, the St. Johns, the Wheelers, the Leeks and the Campbells—for your tireless support and prayers.

To my wonderful family—Mom, Buford, Dad, Whitney, Nanny and Patty, Randy, Tracy, Kimberly and Delana—for once again standing firm through good and bad.

To my beautiful girls—Sarai Grace, Juli Anna and Emma Leigh—for being the best reason a person could have for waking up each morning.

To my wife, Pokey, for being the sweetest voice a person could hear on the first day of the rest of his life.

And to Jesus . . . what can I say that You don't already know? Your tears tell me everything.

PREFACE

As a person living with HIV and AIDS, my entire life has been a race . . . a race against illness and disease, against fear and uncertainty, against discrimination and prejudice. A race against time. Yes, "race" is a good metaphor for what, at times, has been a difficult journey with many twists and turns—from growing up a hemophiliac to discovering my HIV status at 16, to watching how the secrecy of my HIV status affected the emotional life of our family and our relationships.

Mine has been a journey marked by spiritual struggles and tension, from watching my denomination wrestle with the decision to ordain me, to being rejected by the first church to which I was appointed as pastor. Not surprisingly, I have suffered great loss and disillusionment, from the loss of dear friends to the disease, to the loss of others to the fear surrounding it.

And no, the journey so far has not been easy, often pushing me to trust beyond what I can see and understand, and even stretching the limits of my faith, not so much in God as in God's people.

Certainly, this is not a path I would have chosen. I am no martyr and I will never be a saint. Oddly enough, so many miles now into this journey, I would also not trade with anyone what I have learned and lived.

Over the years, I have been asked to speak to groups to share my story, to make real for them what my life has been like as a Christian minister living with HIV/AIDS. Invariably, following each talk, people gather to ask many questions. Some have to do with the everyday details of living with HIV or dealing with chronic illness. Other questions concern my family and how this journey has affected our emotions and relationships. And some questions are more personal and touch upon my health, intimacy and, most fascinating to some, how I can be the father of three healthy daughters.

But the one question, from the moment it was first asked, that has intrigued me and shaped my reflection most is, *What have you learned from living as an HIV-positive person?* Of course, their question and my understanding of it are not the same. Most people are asking about how my life has been shaped by a biological, physical condition. However, I have come to view my medical condition, quite simply, as the doorway through which I take hold of something more valuable—something that shapes my spiritual landscape, affects my view of people, influences my relationships and frames how I view God.

Certainly, my answers to these questions have matured over the years. No longer do I view what God has shown me through this disease as static, but as more of a process, just as is living with the effects of the disease. I don't have one grand scope of God's plan, nor do I see or even look for the "big picture" any longer. Maybe I should, but at what cost? If I were busy trying to make sense of my circumstances, I doubt that I would notice how HIV has provided me with an incredible glimpse into life—into the best of what God offers in this world and the best of what God's people can become. This journey has shown me God's calling for each of us to respond faithfully as God's children and has taught me important lessons that, if all who call ourselves "Christian" learn as well, could change our world. Everyone's journey can do this, if we let it (because don't you learn and live through a tapestry of lives, including yours, others' and God's?).

"Lessons?" you ask.

You bet! Life is learned not from a classroom or study, but from living, sometimes with blessings and opportunities, but more often from struggles and challenges. And it is not a one-time thing. No, the learning does not stop; it is a daily event. We just have to keep showing up.

Lessons?

Yes! Let me give you some examples of what my journey has taught me.

Lessons about *time*. Because of my illness, I am reminded each day that time is a privilege given to us by God, a luxury afforded to us along with the possibility that each of us can make a difference in this world.

Lessons about *relationships*. I am blessed with a beautiful wife, three wonderful daughters, and countless family members and friends who remind me that the most important things we do in this world are not done alone.

Lessons about *simplicity*. "More," "bigger" and "nicer" pale in comparison to simple things like sunsets with those you love and the laughter of children at play.

And most importantly, lessons about real *faith*. Personally, HIV reminds me every day that, with God's grace, what I need, I have—and what I have is sufficient. Sufficient to confront the health struggles of today and the uncertainties of tomorrow; sufficient to meet the needs of others if we, the Body of Christ, agree to meet them together. For still, more than anything I have ever known, the Body of Christ, with all of its imperfections, holds as the hope of the world (when we truly live like it), bearing witness to this amazing gospel that says God passionately loves the unlovable, the marginalized and the forgotten— oh, and by the way, that means we are to love them, too!

I am not saying HIV is easy for any of us. There have certainly been times when I have felt the emptiness and desolation of a seemingly God-less landscape. But the truth is, I have never been alone there, no matter how isolated the path has appeared. This path, this journey, offers real lessons for real life—and if I listen carefully, it teaches me much about loving God and loving others.

Your journey is no different. Maybe you have made mistakes in your life that seem irreparable or unforgivable. Maybe mistakes have been made against you that are too difficult to forgive or forget. Possibly the road has been so smooth that you have missed the lessons because it has been easier to enjoy the good life. Or maybe life has been so messy and uncomfortable that all you have wanted to do is get on with the next chapter. I hear you. But more importantly, God hears you, too.

Misery is not all we are supposed to know . . .

Living in *Miseri* . . . Abiding in Possibility

Abide in me as I abide in you.
Just as the branch cannot bear fruit by itself, unless it abides in the vine,
neither can you, unless you abide in me.

JOHN 15:4, *RSV*

I dwell in Possibility—
A fairer House than Prose—
More numerous of Windows—
Superior—for Doors—
Of Chambers as the Cedars—
Impregnable of Eye—
And for an Everlasting Roof
The Gambrels of the Sky—
Of Visitors—the fairest—
For Occupation—This—
The spreading wide my narrow Hands
To gather Paradise—

EMILY DICKINSON

By 2010, it is estimated that there will be upward of 40 million AIDS orphans in sub-Saharan Africa. This is a stunning figure—one that is almost impossible to fathom. To comprehend the worldwide effects of this pandemic is to lose the ability to stay neutral or even objective. HIV/AIDS is *the* global Pandora's Box that has already been opened and will eventually affect everyone on the planet in one way or another. It already impacts our national security as well as the global economy.

Recently I watched as one commentator spoke of the incredible difficulty of effectively confronting this disease. For every step forward we take in the fight against HIV/AIDS, two more hurdles appear. We provide medicines for 800,000 new patients, only to discover that 3 million new infections have been reported. Yes, when we ponder the nature of this disease, it is overwhelming and invariably begs the question, *What, if anything, can solve such a seemingly impossible problem?*

Not long ago, at the invitation of Rick and Kay Warren, I spoke at the Global AIDS Summit held at Saddleback Community Church in Orange County, California. Amid the amazing array of speakers, professionals and experts, I determined that the Church, both local and global, is our most potent weapon against the HIV/AIDS pandemic. The Church possesses the greatest mobilization, distribution and motivation potential of any institution on Earth. The idea of one billion-plus Christians reaching together into the abyss of this unbelievable struggle captivated my imagination.

But as I reflected further, I became convinced that it is more than the organizational possibilities of the Church that makes the Body of Christ so vital in this fight. As with confronting any impossible problem, the answer for how effectively we fight and how well we succeed lies deeper than just the sound principles that are the basis of any well-run institution. No, such answers begin in simple—and many times, overlooked—places.

A Child Who Sleeps in *Miseri*

A friend of mine recently traveled to Kenya to visit a day orphanage for children who have lost parents to the HIV/AIDS crisis. In Kenya, as in other nations in sub-Saharan Africa, the needs created by the pandemic have overrun the institutional services, especially those that serve children. Day orphanages exist as a means of providing basic necessities to those little ones who would otherwise have nothing—truly a last resort for these "least of these" among us.

Arriving at the orphanage, my friend met two workers carrying a small girl. Her body was frail and clearly malnourished, but her face wore the most beautiful smile. Whereas her body revealed every sign of what is most disturbing and troubling about the plight of those in her situation, her face revealed a spirit that was anything but hopeless.

As these contrasting images collided in my friend's mind, she greeted the young child with the help of an interpreter. My friend learned that the child's father had died just after she was born; her mother died when she was three. She lived with an aunt who was also sick and who could not provide much in the way of care. In fact, the child told my friend that *she* cared for her aunt at night, trying to provide her with as much comfort as possible. Like so many in similar circumstances, this child's was a long, lonely existence.

However, every morning, the workers arrived in a "goat cart" and took her to the day orphanage. Here she found not only food and an occasional change of clothes, but also friends and others with whom she could talk and play. Sure, the toys were few, the meals meager and the clothes secondhand, but this place in the daylight seemed worlds away from her home at night, and it provided what previously appeared impossible: glimpses of hope.

My friend listened intently as the workers and the little girl described her daily routine. "We pick her up," they said in their broken English, "and bring her here so that she might find a little food, some clothes and some schooling. It is not much, but it is more than she has when she returns to *Miseri*."

"Where?" my friend asked, not sure that she had heard right.

"*Miseri*," the worker replied. "It is the name of her settlement. The word comes from the Swahili for 'Egypt.'"

My friend realized that although she had not heard our English word "misery," it certainly conveyed the right meaning. "Misery" was more than appropriate to describe the child's life. After all, what hope did she have? She most likely would not grow up to finish school, train for a job, have a family, or for that matter, enjoy an abundant childhood like the kids my friend knew in the States. No, the chances of her having a future were those same impossible odds the disease brings to everyone who suffers from it—but, for my friend, these obstacles were all the more tragic because now they had a face.

Standing there, my friend was lost in thought, musing on how impossible it all seemed for this little girl. *Where was God? Where was hope? What could effectively confront the wake of this disease, not only for this child but also for all children? What could possibly fill the void left by such desolation of not only a child's present but also her future?* She paused a moment, lost in the realization of such sorrow. But then, as she looked up, she again saw the child's smile and the embrace of the workers, their love and care for this little one. Above all, she saw that in spite of the obvious struggles, this picture seemed full of possibilities, not because the circumstances she had encountered weren't daunting, but because there was something tangibly hopeful about the scene. Surrounded by so much sorrow and despair, my friend saw something amazing—and she found the answer to her questions.

Her answer was right in front of her, resting in what she had almost missed. My friend realized that despite the disease and the impossible circumstances intended for this child, nothing was set in stone. *No.* Why? Because of these people who loved like Jesus, touched like Jesus, cared like Jesus—who had become Jesus to her—*misery* was not all she would know.

What Happens When . . .

This book is about genuine, life-altering hope in Jesus. Not just a recounting of healings and miracles, but a real conversation about real people with real problems—problems that have, for one reason or another, convinced us of a desperation, void of solution or possibility for repair. Sure, sometimes we crave the lessons of our childhood Sunday School, but they seem insufficient in the face of certain situations. This book is about something more than easy answers to difficult questions.

Of course, like many people, I read Scripture either looking for easy answers or only willing to ask the easy questions. (Why wouldn't we?) Truth be told, I like the "feel good" stories the best—you know, when God shows up, does some "divine magic" and then moves on to the next challenge. Lepers at the city gates, the blind and the paralytic—their stories, even with their extremely difficult details, seem neat and clean as Jesus fixes the problem. Yes, I confess: I like the stories in Scripture where people see Jesus coming with their eyes (or at least their spirits) open, where their faith is the only ticket needed and where each lesson can be summarily wrapped in a nice, tidy parable.

I like these accounts because this is the way I like and want my faith to be. Unfortunately, that is not real life, or at least not life as I have come to know it.

Before we go any further, let me assure you that I am not saying these stories don't resonate or speak to our faith. But too often, our tendency is to stuff Scripture into manageable packages, until everything is complicated when the road gets a little too bumpy, or the way a little too long.

When that happens, we end up treating Jesus like the newest spiritual antibiotic. We read our Bibles, sing our songs and pray our prayers long enough to make our pleas before God and give Him our laundry lists of wants and needs, only to slip again, forget again, "not need" again. Sure, we shed a few tears, wring our hands and kneel to pray, usually only long enough to allow the storm to pass and for the winds to subside.

But (you had to know it was coming!) what happens when the storm does not pass? When the pain does not stop? When the prodigal does not return? When the longings won't go away? When we continue to make the same mistakes and break the same hearts? When our sins continue to taunt us? When children continue to die? When the distance between what we do and what God intends widens until we can't even see the other side? When our consciences once again go silent so as to not wake our demons? Friend, let me ask you, for I have asked it myself: *What happens when we can't find even a trace of God . . . when He seems to have disappeared?*

It can happen overnight, before we know what's hit us. Often the tide of doubt and grief and misery rushes in more quickly than we can imagine, and everything in its path is susceptible to its power and rage. It even appears that God must have vanished beneath the waves.

Just ask my friend Sarah what happens when the water comes pouring in.

Storm Surge

Sarah's life had never been easy. Her path to marriage, motherhood and ministry always seemed battered by life's many storms. Her first marriage eroded as a result of a variety of missteps that left her a single mother of three children, struggling to make ends meet. Her second marriage, to a fellow minister, seemed a better fit, although the tension of balancing her first family with a second one compounded the normal and expected challenges of any relationship.

Sarah was also a dedicated minister whose calling to the pastorate provided both an outlet and energy for all the gifts that God had placed within her. She understood the plight of those in need and especially enjoyed the pastorates most unwanted by other pastors, where God would place her to care for those previously forgotten. Like the people living in the inner city of Dallas, Texas—people who didn't speak her language and, in the beginning, could not understand why a 5'11" attractive, brunette, white woman would move her family to their neighborhood. But, like her life, Sarah understood her ministry outside traditional norms. She saw life as an opportunity to see the best in God's people, even if the best could only be viewed from the edge, where few others were willing to go.

Just a few years into her new marriage, Sarah's family moved to the shores of southern Louisiana, where she and her husband each served churches located within a few miles of each other. It was a return home for her husband, who had moved to Texas after their marriage as a means of providing stability for their new family. But urban Texas had proven itself to be no place to raise their children.

Still, her community here was much like that of inner-city Dallas: a mixture of cultures and a clash of economic realities. It also possessed the same scarcity of resources and near-sighted vision that so often plague a people whom prosperity ignores. Yet here Sarah knew she had the opportunity to provide a real-life look at God to people who had otherwise become marginalized by many local congregations. Little did she know, her real challenge had not yet begun.

Early on the morning of August 29, the first bands of a serious hurricane came ashore, but they certainly did not seem to herald the end of the world. However, by evening, the latter seemed not only possible but probable: Hurricane Katrina hit the gulf coasts of Louisiana and Mississippi with Category 3 winds and a record storm surge that transcended anything residents had witnessed in prior hurricanes (even the famed Hurricane Camille

could not compare to Katrina's fierce attack). By the end of the
day, thousands were dead. Millions of residents—the lucky ones—
were without power; countless others had nothing at all and
lacked even the basic necessities of life. On the Mississippi Gulf
Coast, most buildings within one mile of the shoreline had been
either heavily damaged or destroyed completely.

By the morning of August 30, Sarah witnessed the magnitude of what was before them. Her church had been destroyed—
only a concrete slab and a pile of rubble remained. Ironically, as
Sarah noted later, the rubble consisted mostly of items that did
not belong to her congregation but to homes and businesses
located hundreds of yards away. Most of her church's hymnals,
pews and the rest landed in a parking lot northwest of the
building's location. To make matters more complicated, the
building was not accessible by car. The one road that remained
passable was reserved for emergency vehicles, leaving residents
to park some three miles away and walk to any destination
within what officials called the primary impact zone.

But the physical devastation that Katrina had wreaked on
Monday was just the beginning. By Thursday, the devastation
was no longer just about physical needs; emotions were frayed
to the limits. People walked around like zombies, unable to comprehend the vastness of what had occurred. Mothers, fathers
and children of all ages moved through the streets searching for
both the necessities of water and food as well as any pieces of
"normal life"—anything such as pictures and other memorabilia
that might have survived the storm. One observer likened the
scene to Hiroshima or Nagasaki after the atomic explosions of
1945. People moved almost in slow motion, wondering if what
they were seeing belonged to reality or to some horror movie in
which they were unfortunate enough to play a part.

As their despair deepened through the week, people continued to search, but now the searching went deeper. People were

looking for meaning—for hope. Yet as the storm of despair and fear rose to the surface, much like the storm surge, residents found themselves surrounded once again by what seemed an insurmountable wall, this time not of water but of grief and loss. Sarah saw this in her community and she felt it in herself. Watching the *misery*, she wondered what, if anything, could meet this deep need.

Sarah also sensed something familiar. Recalling her ministry in the inner city, she recognized the unmistakable looks of hopelessness. Sarah had seen the blank stares and hollow eyes of people who questioned the intentions of others and the possibilities of a world that seemed to have forgotten them. Time and again, Sarah had watched families struggle under the storm of poverty, abuse and neglect—certainly not the same as the devastation wrought by a hurricane, but no less destructive. And, time and again, she found the simple offering of herself and her faith as the only remedy, the only way to bring relief.

When Sunday came, Sarah did not have a church building, but she was keenly aware that she still had a congregation—maybe not the same worshipers as before, because now her church was made up of those the world had made the "least of these." These worshipers were still searching on this Sunday morning, searching for food, water, clothes and for deeper things that would soothe their souls. So, as morning dawned on this day of rest, Sarah did what she had done before the storm—she got up and made her way to what used to be her church building, in search of the Body of Christ. She parked near the boundaries of the impact zone, got out of her car and began to walk. She walked for three miles, past downed trees and power lines, piles of rubble, broken homes and shattered lives. She walked past the all-too-familiar markings of orange paint and the barricades. And she walked past memories and into the stories of hurting people, forgotten people and missing people. She walked until she found herself on the concrete slab of the sanctuary and then waited for her congregation to arrive, unsure if anyone would show, but determined that, on this Sunday, on this site, the Church was open for business.

As people gathered—some friends, some strangers, all wandering and wondering—they began to sing and speak the words of grace. They hugged and reminisced about common and not-so-common stories, and they cried and mourned what used to be. By the end of their time together, much longer than their regular church service would have lasted, they joined hands and shared communion, not as some ritual of obligation, but as a promise that the God who had carried them through the storm would see them through this difficult and eerie calm.

As Sarah finished praying with the last person on that Sunday morning, she pictured in her mind what had been taken from her community so quickly and tragically. But she also saw what had not been stolen by this storm—the hope of the Body of Christ and the promise that where the people gather, God is in their midst. She realized that this storm was only a footnote in the journey—a powerful impression, mind you—but simply a footnote. And she guessed that all storms in all journeys were footnotes to the greater meaning of it all.

With that, this wife, mother and minister moved toward the street and again started to walk. Not many steps down the road, she turned and looked back at the concrete slab and the makeshift altar and cross. Taking it in, she saw something she had not seen in what seemed months, although it had only been a few days. Sarah saw hope, not in the structure that once was, but in a place and a people, who, for a moment, talked about Jesus . . . sang about Jesus . . . and loved like Jesus. In that instant, Sarah knew that, in this journey, none of them was alone.

I am not sure the worldly observer would call Sarah's life exceptional. I can't be certain that anyone would seek her opinion or advice on significant matters. I am not even sure if the people to whom Sarah ministered truly appreciated who she was in their midst. But what I do know is that Sarah's life and story caused me to stop and to think about storms and about God's people and how the two, oftentimes, connect. She made me pause and reflect on how far I would walk either physically or spiritually on the chance that someone might need to hear a word of grace, or might need to just have someone else show up. Sarah's life caused me to hope and to believe that God understands our journeys, whether along those three miles of devastation or throughout life. To God, nothing is too lost or too far gone to be found or restored. He has the power to change the flood of despair, hopelessness and misery into, once again, life's deep well of possibility.

Finding God

A friend once told me that God is not afraid of our doubts, our questions or our anger. What God does not like is when we turn away and think we can do this on our own. And His sadness deepens when we believe that our journey is just somehow too screwed up to have any redemptive meaning. Why does this sadden God so? Because He knows the need for the *journey*.

Think about the life and death of Jesus: Have you ever wondered why Jesus had to be born, live through a pretty normal life, launch a ministry and *then* provide for the salvation of the world? God didn't just rectify some cosmic, spiritual debt (please excuse me, but God could have mailed that payment in). No, God knew the power of the journey and so became like us, took on a story Himself, to show us that through *everything* there is a reason to survive, something to hope for and something to learn.

Before Jesus, the people of God understood the journey from only one angle: God was *up there* (in the sky, in the fire, on a mountain, in the Temple) and they were *down here*. Calvary changed that. There, the story got personal for God—and for you and me. Just take a look at Jesus' last words on the cross:

> *Father, forgive them* . . . (Luke 23:34).
> *Why have you forsaken Me?* . . . (Matt. 27:46).
> *Take care of My mother* . . . (John 19:26-27).
> *I am thirsty* . . . (John 19:28).
> *I am through with this* . . . (John 19:30).

Do those prayers sound familiar to you? They do to me. Why? Because in one form or another, I have prayed them, too. Haven't you?

Reading those words reminds me that Jesus knows what it is like to hurt, to care about others, to be frustrated, to feel forgotten and to be exhausted. And, if Jesus knows all of these things, then He must also know what it is like to wonder if the whole journey is worth it (*Oh, that's right, the Garden of Gethsemane*) or what it is like to lose a loved one (*Yes, I remember Jesus cried for Lazarus*) or what it is like to feel betrayed and forgotten (*Did you just think about Judas?*).

Jesus knows what it's like.

God knows a few things, too. God knows really big projects, like how to cause *really big bangs!* God knows complicated projects, like how to separate light from dark (think about being the first to confront that issue). God knows the solutions to tough dilemmas, like how to reconcile justice and righteousness with unconditional love.

But let me share with you other things that the God of infinite power and knowledge knows . . . God knows what it is like to hurt, both on the inside and outside. God knows what it is like to lose people you love. God knows what it is like to keep saying the same thing and feel as if no one is listening. God knows what it is like to give away with little hope of receiving anything in return. God knows about family and friends. God knows comfortable places like a mother's embrace, cool places like a riverbed, and barren, forgotten places like a wilderness and a hill made of jagged rock.

God also knows that things are not lost, just unfound. God knows that tough situations have deeper meanings. God knows that creation comes from chaos and that hope comes from struggle. God knows that one step does not the whole journey make.

Oh, and one other thing . . . the most important thing . . . the unforgettable thing . . . the most incredible thing: God knows *you* and God knows *me*, and that is our new beginning and our hope. Not a hope that we will take the journey perfectly in step, with every missing piece in place and no mistakes made, but a hope that, because God knows the way, where we've been will mean something before the journey is done. For even when God seems to have disappeared, His work to redeem our misery into possibility goes on.

I am not sure where or when you are reading this book, but I'm glad you are. Sit back and relax. Find your favorite drink or snack and plan to stay awhile. I don't know where your life is at this moment, but I know that God has something amazing in store for you, not because of any words that I could write, but because God desperately wants you to see that no life is beyond restoring, no misery so great that it does not hold within it the possibility of redemption. If this book is the vehicle by which restoration and redemption happen, *so be it* . . . but this journey is not about me—or even you. No, as the life of Jesus shows us again and again, especially as we watch certain encounters unfold in Scripture, the journey is about *us*, together with Him.

Along the way, I will introduce you to friends and acquaintances like Sarah who have made an impact on my journey.

Hopefully, through their stories, you will see the incredible, working presence of God in each of us. Of course, I will share glimpses from my own story, and just maybe you will gain a sense of why living for Jesus means so much to me. But most important for both of us, I will share His story, and while I am writing and you are reading it, we will once again see why faith in Him is not in vain.

So, friend, what do you say? Shall we find Him together?

1

The First Encounter: Zacchaeus

LUKE 19:1-10

If I wait for immaculate, I will never have a guest.
LAUREN F. WINNER, *MUDHOUSE SABBATH*

On the advice of a friend, I have gathered around me a group of people I call my Initial Readers, or IRs for short. They are professors, mechanics, English teachers and doctors who read what I write and give me honest (sometimes brutal) feedback. When I mentioned my idea for this book about God's love for those who feel hopeless or close to it, each of my IRs enthusiastically supported the effort. However, when they discovered that Zacchaeus was included as one of the examples, my IRs questioned the choice.

"You mean the story of the short man who climbs the tree?" one friend asked.

"The guy from my daughter's *Children's Storybook Bible*?" another IR inquired.

My IRs, like many of us, have read the story of Zacchaeus from one of two angles, seeing him as either the "wee little" man who can't get a glimpse of Jesus or as the tax collector hated by everyone in town. But to go further into his story is to discover an amazing, and possibly unsettling, family resemblance.

Read the story of Zacchaeus in Luke's Gospel as though it is the first time you have encountered it, and you might be surprised at what you find: Zacchaeus is familiar to us because each of us can identify with some part of his struggle. We see ourselves in him. Here is a man torn and conflicted, caught between the standards of this world and the desire for something deeper. Zacchaeus has relational problems, physical struggles and a spiritual sorrow that causes him to do irrational things. He is filled with internal conflict, guilt about past wrongs and a strong desire to somehow turn back the clock and make it all better. But manipulating time works no better for Zacchaeus than it does for us, and he is left in an almost hopeless state. Zacchaeus is out of control, out of plans and out of ideas. And so it is that he finds himself sitting in a tree alongside a dusty road, waiting for the Man from Nazareth to come by.

Zacchaeus's story cuts close to home. We see glimpses of ourselves, for we have all fought at least one or two of Zacchaeus's battles. We have all made decisions that create confusion and trouble in our lives, and we have all wished that somehow, some way, we could turn back the clock and do it over again.

Yes, Zacchaeus is more than a Bible story about a wee little man. His story is about every man and woman—tall or short, large or small—who has found life desperately wanting and is in need of something new. And his questions resonate deeply with the desperate place in all of us: *How? Could He? Why should He? What's the use?*

So, no—I don't believe that Zacchaeus's story is at all out of place in a book about desperate people finding hope when God seems to have disappeared. It may be more *our story* than any of us knew.

All Trash Goes to the Street, Part One

Growing up, one of my household chores included taking the garbage to the street. It was mundane and laborious, but without it our home filled quickly with trash. Not to say that we were slobs, but it was amazing how much garbage our little family of four could produce.

The routine of getting the trash to the street played the same every week: I combed the house, emptying all of the smaller garbage cans into a larger bag that I then took to the metal receptacle (a fancy name for the trash bin) out back. It didn't matter if the smaller cans were nearly empty; on garbage day, every can was checked and received a new bag. I'm not sure of the necessity for this unbendable standard, except the knowledge that on this day our house was to be completely trash free.

After emptying the large bag into the metal trash can, it was time to get the can to the street. I grew up in the days before trash cans had wheels, so I had to either carry the entire can to the street (no small feat, given that it was metal and cumbersome) or drag it. The latter was dangerous because of the possibility that the can might turn over, dumping everything, from old candy wrappers, to souring milk jugs, to decaying fruit and to dirty diapers, everywhere. All the while I dragged the can, I understood that if the unthinkable did happen, I would have to pick up the mess. Needless to say, I was careful, perhaps painfully so, as I maneuvered the trash to the street. I didn't want anyone to see our garbage, and I certainly didn't want to touch it! Thankfully, most weeks were uneventful and the garbage made it safely to the corner. Still, each trip was a harrowing adventure.

Of course, there were other variables that came into play on garbage day. Rain was always a problem. I mean, water and garbage—need I say more? Then there was the possibility of an inordinate amount of trash, say from a birthday party or cookout, that required bringing out the "extra can"—which was actually the *old* can, which was beaten and rusty and just one drag away from the bottom falling out. This didn't happen all at once but gradually along a 20-yard swath that left a stream of trash in its wake. Not pretty.

But the greatest unknown was whether the neighbor's dog would jump the less-than-well-built fence and make a mid-morning snack from our family's leftover Jell-O and chicken (no, they didn't start off as part of the same dish). Rottweilers are neither neat nor discriminating—this particular pooch usually spread the buffet across our front yard and down the street. And because our neighborhood lived by the "It doesn't matter where the garbage lands; if it's yours, pick it up" rule, I spent a lot of time combing the block to retrieve my purloined rubbish. (The Rottweiler disappeared after my sophomore year in high school. Some say he ran away, but I suspect foul play—he disappeared the day after garbage day.)

Although much has changed in my life, the ritual of getting garbage to the street continues to this day. I am now married and the father of three daughters (who, by the way, have never taken out the trash). But my job is now much easier. Thankfully, some saint-in-the-making put wheels on trash cans and thought to make them plastic (I bet that he or she had a trash-loving dog, or at least a neighbor who did). And I can't say enough about trash can lids that actually fit and stay in place. Genius, pure genius!

Over the years, I have wondered about the whole process of taking out the trash. I mean, who actually thought of that? And who decided that trash should go to the street? What did people do before trash removal? Oh, yeah . . . they lived in it.

When I really think about it, I like our system; it makes sense. We bring our trash to the street because it is cleaner and easier (not to mention healthier) for the sanitation professionals to help us dispose of it. Their deal with us is simple: *You bring it to the corner and we will take care of the rest. No, we won't go get it for you—that's your job—but you are not in this alone.*

Spiritual Sanitation

When it comes to getting rid of our spiritual trash, we are not alone—but we also have to do our part. Sadly, learning how to get our trash to the curb can be a long process for some people. Case in point, the husband of a friend of mine—let's call him "Bob."

Bob

Though Bob is pathologically unfaithful to his wife, by all other accounts he is a nice guy. He is a good provider, an excellent father and a regular at church. That said, the altar is a familiar place for him. When Bob's knees hit the altar pads, everyone knows that he has, once again, fallen off the wagon and onto a flight attendant or bar companion.

From one angle, Bob is simply a liar and cheat. That's your opinion, too? It's not hard to reach that conclusion. Bob *is* the problem. His transgressions bring enormous confusion and pain not only to his marriage but also to his children, extended family and friends. And worse, the pattern is always the same: He goes months without any slip-ups, only to suddenly find himself looking at an attractive woman across the brim of a Jack Daniels and Coke or a champagne glass, which inevitably leads to a less-than-meaningful encounter. Afterward, he is always sorrowful, sad and penitent—and he swears that it will never happen again.

But it always happens one more time. Many of us have advised our friend to leave her husband; Bob obviously cares more about his appetite for destruction than for the significant relationships in his life. We grow sad and tired of watching the downward spiral time and again, and as far as many are concerned, Bob carries around too much emotional garbage ever to change.

Several days after the last episode, Bob arrived in my office. Clearly out of options, he sought more solace than answers.

He knew where I stood concerning his marriage, and he believed that his wife might change her mind about leaving if I were to so advise. (Bob overestimated my ability to influence her, either to leave or to stay.)

We discussed his situation in depth, and although my words were neither comforting nor reassuring (I kept thinking, *How many times do you watch this before you simply wash your hands?*), the longer I listened to Bob, the deeper I saw into his nature and actions. Quite honestly, I was not prepared for what I saw. In talking about his habitual patterns and why they seemed so hard to break, I discovered that Bob had come from a broken home and had an abusive father. He had been the target of verbal and physical abuse from the age of eight and had never developed a sense of healthy self-esteem. Not surprisingly, Bob descended into a pattern of self-loathing that made good things almost impossible to accept, or at least hold on to for any period of time. Bob's deep-seated need for approval, even from inappropriate sources, fed a craving in him that, gone unchecked, had surfaced time and again.

Bob had a lot of trash in his life that he had simply pushed deep within. He refused to let anyone help him, even his wife, and thus he used these unhealthy behavior patterns as a way of self-medicating his guilt, shame and pain. Yes, he knew what he was doing was wrong, but he felt powerless against temptation.

While Bob could clearly identify the trash in his life, he could only stuff it, moment to moment, into a dark corner of his hurting soul. No one had shown him how to bag it and get it to the street. Over time, it was easier for Bob to let the unhealthy pattern win, reminding me that, many times, getting healthy hurts more than suffering from the disease. Bob discovered that, as the trash mounts, life becomes septic and our sense of a better way becomes paralyzed.

Tara

Fortunately, not everyone who has trash in their life lets it fester; some people have learned how to get it to the curb and out of their way. Tara was just such a person. I met her while I was waiting to see the doctor at our local hematology/oncology clinic.

As a hemophiliac who had just had major surgery, I made daily visits to the clinic to check the status of my clotting levels. Although the visits were inconvenient—daily for almost five weeks—they were simple and required little more than a blood test each time. For most of the others in the waiting room, however, the visits meant life and death. The clinic served primarily cancer patients, and being in their presence over those weeks humbled me as I watched each of them face their battles. Whenever I was filled with all sorts of self-pity, I would think of the folks I met in that waiting room, people like Mary who had pelvic cancer, Roger who had bone cancer, Jake with non-Hodgkin's lymphoma, or Gail with cancer of the pancreas. I did more than wait in that waiting room . . . I gained perspective.

Perhaps no one gave me more—and better—perspective than Tara. She sat across from me in the waiting room one day and chatted with anyone who was willing. She looked young, far too young to be in that place, but I had learned over the course of those weeks that cancer knows no age limits. Tara was tall and attractive with an electric smile and outgoing personality. I learned later that she was 23 years old, married and the mother of a beautiful 2-year-old girl.

A year earlier, on her daughter's first birthday, Tara learned that she had throat cancer. Although doctors had caught the disease early and believed a full recovery was possible, the shock of such news at a young age, together with all the cares of family and motherhood, made the news overwhelming. And getting the bad news was just the beginning. Tara's treatment included several months of both radiation and chemotherapy.

She lost her hair as well as her taste for food. She used a central port (a medical device that keeps a vein open for injections) for nutritional supplements and for her chemo treatments. Needless to say, hers had not been a pleasant journey.

It was no surprise that Tara found balancing treatment, motherhood and her job at a local law firm almost impossible at times. She wondered whether or not it was all worth it—whether the treatments would work and, most importantly, whether her emotional strength could hold out.

But, remarkably, after enduring so many treatments and walking more than her share of hard roads, she sat in front of me laughing and talking. It was now one year later, and Tara was cancer free. Her hair had grown back, and she happily shared with me the details about the first meal she had eaten after her sense of taste returned: fried catfish, French fries and hush puppies.

As I listened to her story, I sat amazed at Tara's maturity and strength. She talked about family and faith in such personal, profound terms. I realized her journey had forced Tara to reflect on life at depths most people never go. She talked about issues with a keener sense than most 40-year-olds, reminding me of the power of serious illness to enrich our relationships and points of view.

Tara was no longer a 22-year-old girl; cancer had transformed her into a 23-year-old veteran of life. She had endured the unbearable and, in the process, given her family a future.

The more I listened to her talk, the way she phrased her words and framed her thoughts, it became clear that she was strong and focused. Watching this amazing young lady, I couldn't help but think how different she was from Bob. Unlike Bob, Tara had no desire to hold on to the garbage of her life—the fear, doubt and uncertainties. Instead, she had learned to pack them up daily and take them to the street, more than happy for others to help carry them away.

Bob and Tara approached life differently. For Tara, addressing her problems and then asking for help meant freedom. For Bob, it meant pain, rejection and a willingness to live in the filth of his decisions rather than take the risk that others might discover his baggage, his imperfections. Tara saw no alternative. She would not give up and would not allow cancer to eat away at her from the inside. On the other hand, Bob lived in fear of the short-term consequences that confession might bring, and so he jeopardized any possibility for long-term healing.

Of course, observers might qualify a comparison of Bob and Tara by pointing out that their lives, difficulties and circumstances are different, and that shame and guilt far outweigh the more noble fight against cancer. *Sure, no one blames Tara for having cancer, but Bob . . . well, he knows better.* But the truth is, whether it is cancer or infidelity, we all must decide to get our garbage to the street. When we don't, we play into Satan's plan: He does not care what the filth is, just as long as he can convince us to hold on to it.

The Wee Little Man

Have you ever wondered what would cause Zacchaeus to make his way to the street? He was clearly not welcome as he weaved in and out of the crowds, trying to catch a glimpse of Jesus. And it wasn't just his physical stature that prevented him from getting close. The crowd despised Zacchaeus and anyone like him who, in their eyes, was defiling the faith. Zacchaeus was the worst kind of pariah—as a tax collector for Rome, his transgression was considered a betrayal of the core of Jewish culture.

As with so many stories in the Bible, the setting for Zacchaeus's encounter with Jesus is certainly no coincidence. Jericho has a familiar history—it was the ancient city that, centuries before, stood between the Israelites and the Promised Land. When Joshua arrived with the Israelites, Jericho was insulated, proud of its ability to keep out the unwanted. Its tumbling walls became the stuff of legend—what child's Bible storybook doesn't include an account of Joshua and his army marching around the city until the walls collapsed upon themselves? The rest, as they say, is history.

By the time of Jesus, it had more than rebounded. Jericho had become a geographic and cultural center of the ancient world, considered a travel hub for getting to Jerusalem and other regions of Palestine. Because of this, trade and commerce thrived in Jericho, making it one of the wealthiest cities of the area and providing its inhabitants with high social status. The Romans valued Jericho because of its tax potential; thus, as a tax collector, Zacchaeus was not just any run-of-the-mill official—he was a prized part of the Roman establishment.

To the Jewish citizens of Jericho, however, Zacchaeus was a traitor. Sure, he had achieved great power and wealth, but at what price? He was one of the most hated men in the city, epitomizing the image of someone who possessed everything but *had* nothing. It was a life of great and painful contrasts: the best of the world's bounty, the worst of the soul's distress.

We know little about Zacchaeus's past, how he grew up or how he rose to the position of tax collector. What we do know is that Zacchaeus, for one reason or another, had chosen this life and, as is often the case with those like him, found himself in a pattern of choices that, over time, offered little in the way of better alternatives.

Still, Zacchaeus sought something different. Maybe he had heard about Jesus and His teachings, about how He loved the sinners and ate with outcasts. Something within Zacchaeus must have liked the idea of what He stood for, and longed for the opportunity to know more about this man named Jesus. Maybe there was enough of a desire for the "other road," the one less traveled, in Zacchaeus that he believed getting a glimpse of Jesus might create a miracle. We'll never know.

Regardless, we find him weaving through the hateful crowd, vying for an opportunity to see the Teacher from Nazareth. Zacchaeus was many miles down a lonesome, twisted road and perhaps believed that Jesus would never associate with him. *But what if He would?* Zacchaeus determined that the risk was worth it, that maybe, unlike what everyone else in that crowd believed, he was not too far gone for something to change.

I believe that all of us, if we listen closely enough, can hear the ring of a new call in our lives. Very few of us get up in the morning, look in the mirror and say, "Today, I will screw up my life!" No, the voice deep within us, no matter how far we have wandered, echoes our longings for new directions and possibilities. So what is the problem? If the voice is speaking, why don't more of us listen and respond? Maybe it is a lack of courage, or perhaps fear of the unknown (*This path may not be good, but at least I know where it leads*). Possibly it is just self-centeredness, the belief that we can or at least should be able to guide the journey ourselves. Or just maybe, we can't get our brains around the possibility that God could love us in this state—that God would accept us like this.

I'm sure Zacchaeus could never have imagined how his day would turn out. Who could? Getting a glimpse of Jesus is one thing; having Him invite Himself to dinner at your house—no way! (But we're getting ahead of ourselves . . .)

Whatever he was thinking that day, however he imagined the outcome, Zacchaeus did the only thing we are asked to do: He made his way to the street, garbage in hand, and waited to see if there was any truth to what he had heard about this Jesus—if someone like Jesus could love someone like him.

A View from the Top

Before we go on with Zacchaeus's story, let's talk for a minute about why we climb trees.

"Because they are there" was Kevin's reason. He lived across the street from me most of my early life. Kevin was shy and quiet. Getting him to talk was a chore—he saved his words for important declarations (such as the one above).

The tree in question was a large pecan tree that sat in the middle of Kevin's front yard. It dominated everything with its sprawling branches that seemed to stretch out over the entire perimeter of the yard. This wasn't just any tree—no, this tree was important to the kids in our neighborhood. It provided shade in the summer, had a great area just beneath its branches for intense marble matches and, most importantly, served as first base in our regular neighborhood baseball games. Of course, it was also a magnet for kids who loved to climb.

Pretty much every kid in the neighborhood tried to climb this tree, which was no easy feat. Pecan trees have tall trunks with branches that start higher up than most trees. Maneuvering your way from the ground to that first branch was an accomplishment in itself. But the tree had an inviting sense about it—it was almost as if a sign that said "Climb me" hung around its trunk. And so, kids climbed as though they were fulfilling a childhood rite of passage. How high you went didn't matter as much as making the attempt. The battle scars of scraped knees and elbows said something about you: that you were not afraid and, more importantly, that you belonged.

As I said, almost everyone had climbed the tree . . . everyone but me. Because I was a hemophiliac, tree climbing was frowned on by almost every adult I knew. For me, scraped knees and bruises meant medicine and trips to the emergency room. Injuries were expensive, not to mention taxing on my parents, who had to rearrange their lives and schedules to take care of me. Getting unavoidably hurt was one thing; getting hurt out of stupidity was quite another.

However, I did my share of childhood rule breaking, from my short stint in Little League to BMX-bike racing to neighborhood football (in full pads). My mother, who always talked tough on the front end, somehow knew that little boys often do what they know they shouldn't, and thus, she handled my childhood with grace and patience. Mom wasn't always happy with my choices, but she always seemed to understand. She knew that part of living with the disease involved my desire to be as normal as everyone else. (Now that I have children, I really don't know how Mom endured my antics. Certainly my tree-climbing attempts in particular must have tested her patience in the extreme.)

I made my first climb up that pecan tree on a spring day when all of the other kids on the street were gone. I stood at its base for several minutes to consider what might be the easiest and least dangerous way up the trunk. Planting my foot in a small indention a couple of feet up from the ground, I grabbed on to a small knot in the bark and began to climb. I was methodical and patient, moving slowly and carefully. When I reached the branches, I stopped and looked around. Then I began again, this time moving more quickly, one branch to another. Finally, I realized that I was out of branches. I had climbed to the very top. Two thoughts raced through my mind. One was amazement at how far I had come. The other was the realization that what goes up must come down.

Thankfully, the trip down was uneventful, but I did receive my share of bruises and scrapes along the way. I knew I would be in trouble when my mother realized what I had done and that I would not see daylight for sometime. But even as my mother reprimanded me, she had a wry smile on her face as though she had climbed a tree or two herself.

Yes, tree climbing landed me at the emergency room, and I had several adults remind me that not only was I a hemophiliac, I was apparently not a very bright one. Yet in spite of the multiple scoldings, I somehow knew it was worth it. It's hard to explain the feeling: I stood at the top of that tree and knew that things were different.

And I realized for the first time that we don't climb trees because the tree is there; we climb because *we* are there.

Soul Weary

Not long ago, I underwent heart bypass surgery. As a person who prided himself on eating right and exercising appropriately, I was shocked by the news of my arterial blockage. The bypass procedure and recovery were painful and emotionally draining. The experience was also spiritually challenging, although I didn't realize until later exactly just how challenging it was.

During the early days of my recovery, I had trouble praying. At first, I thought I was tired or just not able to think clearly, courtesy of my various pain medications. However, after arriving home from the hospital, I wrote two articles for my newspaper column with relative ease and realized that my cognitive state was not to blame for my lack of prayer. The problem was not physiological; it was me. Yes, I was tired physically, but I had no idea how weary I was in my soul.

The road had been an exhausting one, starting on the day doctors discovered the blockage, only days prior to the surgery. Tests had revealed a serious lesion in one of the main arteries to the heart. To do nothing was certain death, but the complexities of my other health conditions made bypass surgery very risky. In the days prior to surgery, I struggled with the very real possibility that I would not survive the procedure.

Surgery was scheduled for the Monday after Easter. And so, on that Easter day, I held my girls close and, in the best way I could, tried to tell them goodbye. In those moments, it is amazing what matters most. I made sure that the material things of my family's life were in order—money, property, life insurance, and so on—but by that afternoon, I focused on my children, wanting them to know how proud I was of them and what a blessing they were to me. I wanted my wife to know how much I loved her, and how much I cherished the years of friendship and joy we had shared. I wanted my mom to know how much I respected her for all she had been through and for all that she had become. I wanted family and friends to laugh with me and know that their joy had made my life complete. During those moments on that Easter afternoon, there was no talk about paperwork or details, just conversations about relationships and what the presence of my family and friends on the journey had meant to me.

Okay, okay . . . I obviously survived the procedure, and I am blessed. But those days prior to surgery reminded me of the fragile nature of this life and of the importance of not taking any moment for granted.

Yet such moments are also draining, and the exhaustion began to grow in my soul. When we are weary in the deepest places of our lives, prayer is often the first thing to go. In times of crisis, most of us pray and are filled with an adrenaline that sustains us. But over time, as the acuteness of the situation subsides, so does the adrenaline. What remains is a place of quiet where the soul-wearied person finds him- or herself going through the motions. Such a spiritual weariness is not caused by apathy, as some have suggested; it goes much deeper than that. It is more of a "watching" feeling—part skepticism, part longing, but without any means to either explain it or make it better. A friend, who understands this feeling all too well, describes it this way: "Soul weariness, when you're there, feels like the last and least place you would ever want to be, but you can't think of anywhere else to go." Exactly.

That is where I found myself in those days following surgery. I could talk *to* God, but not *with* Him. And, at first, the one-way conversation was filled with harshness and anger. I talked in tones of moral indignation and self-righteousness that now, in retrospect, make me wince. But I kept talking—and, strangely enough, God didn't seem to mind. I never had a sense that God was mad at me or uncomfortable with my tone. No, even through my ranting, I had a picture of God waiting, waiting on me to let it all out, before He would finally speak.

When God did speak, His voice came through strange ways and in unexpected places. I first heard God in the voice of an elderly lady down the street who walks her dog every morning. As I strolled along with my pillow clutched to my chest, I passed the lady. In all the times that I have seen her walking, we had never spoken except to wave or smile. On this day, she stopped, looked at the pillow and said, "If nothing else, this time of your life will show you what to hold on to." She was talking about the pillow, but I heard a more poignant meaning.

In another moment, God's voice came from a child who was asked one Saturday what he would like to do. He replied, "Let's go see Mr. Shane; it will do me good just to look at him." I had never realized this little boy liked me that much. God's voice came from family and friends who patiently reminded me that I was not alone in this journey and whose encouragement refreshed, time and again, my tired heart. Finally, God's voice came from the waiting room of the cancer center, where people much worse off than I was offered prayer and support *for me*. Their witness and support reminded me of faith in a God who loves us *because* of our imperfections and weakness, not just in spite of them. Weary in soul as I was, I rested secure in Him.

When I think of Zacchaeus, I think of a weary soul. Sure, his condition was not the same as mine, but it was still life-threatening and soul-draining. Zacchaeus made his way to the street because he was tired of hurting. He was tired of his life, knowing that no matter how many things he accumulated, he would still feel empty. Zacchaeus was sad about not knowing his neighbors and even sadder that his neighbors thought they knew him. His broken heart pushed him to the street, garbage in hand, hoping that on this day, just maybe something would give, and something in his life could change.

But getting to the street was only the beginning; he then had to fight his way through the crowd. Their anger was real but not entirely their fault. He knew he had helped plant it in their hearts. He was not innocent in this; they had every right to hate him—and I'm sure the Adversary loved reminding him of that. But Zacchaeus kept walking, kept shouting back at the whisper of doubt inside him and kept looking through the crowd to see if Jesus had arrived.

At that moment, Zacchaeus must have felt hopeless. Soul weary. Human nature says, *Turn around. Why try? You'll never make it through the crowd. They won't let you!* But then Zacchaeus saw the tree, and he began to climb. He climbed more quickly and farther than he could have imagined. He climbed because he was there, and the tree gave him a chance to belong to something better than what he had known before.

"If I wait for immaculate, I will never have a guest," writes Lauren F. Winner. Certainly Zacchaeus couldn't wait for immaculate, couldn't wait for everything to be perfect. Time was working against him, and the Guest was coming around the corner. So what if they made fun of him for climbing a tree to get a glimpse of Jesus? Zacchaeus knew the crowd would not miraculously part. No, this was as perfect as it would ever be.

All Trash Goes to the Street, Part Two

Several weeks following the devastating impact of Hurricane Katrina, a friend of mine traveled to the Gulf Coast of Mississippi to survey the damage. What he found was beyond anything he could have imagined. Entire neighborhoods no longer existed. Businesses had been destroyed. Countless lives had been lost. My friend described the scene as "apocalyptic."

While driving through one particular subdivision on his way to a local church, my friend noticed the stacks of debris near the street in front of each house. The piles were enormous and included every household good imaginable, from clothes to appliances to boxes of personal items. But he could not help but notice how neat and organized the piles were compared to those on the other streets he had seen. This neighborhood street seemed out of place, given the destruction and chaos that reigned everywhere else. This neighborhood had experienced the same calamity of water and wind, but their recovery was different.

As my friend looked closer at each pile, another fact stood out: On each pile was written the name of the family who lived in that particular house. At that moment, he saw a resident of the neighborhood dragging more debris to the street. My friend stopped and asked if he could help. The gentleman politely declined and turned back toward the house.

My friend stopped him and asked, "Sir, can I ask you a question?"

"Yes, what is it?" the gentleman replied.

My friend pointed to the piles of debris and said, "It's about your debris piles. They seem organized and neat, and I can't help but notice that each pile has a name on it. Would you tell me about that?"

The gentleman stood a moment looking at the piles. "We've always been a close neighborhood. Most of us have lived here for years—we've raised our children here, lived and died here . . . it's been a good place."

The man paused a minute and then continued. "Notice came from the recovery folks that we needed to drag 'all trash to the street.' Not everyone has come back yet, but many did, and so we began cleaning up the neighborhood. We started with our own homes, but took time to help each other, and we all pitched in to clean up the homes of those who couldn't make it back. Eventually, we got all the trash away from the houses and to the street, like they asked."

The man stopped, pointed toward the debris and piles, and said, "We loved our homes and we loved our neighborhood. We realized as we began the cleanup that we weren't just throwing trash to the street; these were our lives we were discarding—pictures, china, memorabilia. We didn't want to just throw it out there and have some stranger pick it up without knowing that every pile represents a life's worth of dreams, heartaches and struggle. That's why we put the name on each pile—so that people would know that this was more than another impact zone . . . this place meant something."

My friend turned to look at the piles and realized that each mound deserved to be owned and cherished, even as they were. The piles may not have looked like much sitting by the street, but by naming them, the neighbors gave value to their struggle.

The debris in our lives is no different. Even as we drag it to the street, each sickness, each conflict, each season of profound darkness can be imbued with value and meaning when its purpose in the longer journey of our lives is named.

The Name-Caller

When Jesus saw Zacchaeus sitting in the tree, He stopped and called him by name: "Zacchaeus, come down. Today, I will eat at your house" (see Luke 19:5). Can you imagine the shock, not only for Zacchaeus, but also for the entire crowd? *Did Jesus just speak to Zacchaeus? Did He just say that He was eating dinner at Zacchaeus's house?* I'm sure the questions and comments rivaled anything our modern gossip experts could generate.

But Jesus knew exactly what He was doing. Let's face it, Jesus is a "name-caller," and the name He likes the most is our own. Throughout the Gospels, we hear of Jesus calling people by name—and not just the religious folks, either. No, Jesus spent time calling the names of people who hadn't heard their names spoken in a welcoming tone in quite a while. Jesus knew the power of giving people dignity in order to later change their lives. It had probably been a long time since someone had called Zacchaeus by name without connecting it to some form of profanity or curse. To hear his name spoken by Jesus, of all people, must have been like hearing beautiful music.

However, Jesus is not only a name-caller. He also likes a good party. We know because He was always inviting Himself to one. And why not? What better place to get to know someone than around a table, sharing a good meal with good friends? Jesus liked to enter into people's space and get to the heart of who they were. He couldn't have cared less about what the religious folks and the social elite thought. Jesus wanted to know the real insides of people so that He could fill those empty places with something of real value.

By calling Zacchaeus's name, Jesus gave Zacchaeus an identity; by going to his home, Jesus gave Zacchaeus a future. Jesus placed a name on the pile of debris called Zacchaeus's life and gave meaning to it all.

Zacchaeus's response surprised those around him, but it shouldn't surprise us. We read the rest of the story and know what happens when sinners encounter the love of Jesus: The change can't be contained. It is overwhelming, and it causes people to do crazy things, like give away their possessions and try to make things right. Zacchaeus did the only thing he could have done. His heart had been opened and he wanted to respond, but not in some token way. No, Zacchaeus exploded in gratitude and thanksgiving. He gave back to those who he had wronged, not once or twice but four times what he owed them. Forgiveness makes people do amazing things because forgiveness is in itself such an amazing act—and the more amazing it feels, the more amazing the response.

Even more wonderful, though, was Jesus' proclamation. After Zacchaeus responded, Jesus declared, "Today, salvation has come to this house, because this man, too, is a son of Abraham" (Luke 19:9). Jesus named Zacchaeus and restored him to the family. Zacchaeus was no longer an outcast or orphan; he belonged. Why did he belong? Because of a profound truth in Jesus' final statement, words that speak to every Zacchaeus everywhere who believes that his or her life has too much garbage for God to ever love him or her. Jesus looked at those gathered around that table and said, "For the Son of Man came to seek and to save what was lost" (Luke 19:10).

Think about that for a minute. Did you hear those two words? *Seek* and *save*. Zacchaeus had never been too far gone or too hopeless to find the love of God. And God didn't want Zacchaeus to miss out on the sweetness of a transformed life.

God calls us to bring our trash to the street, to 'fess up to our deception, face our wrongs and claim our sin. But all the while, God is there, seeking after us, guiding us and showing us the way. We may not see or even know it, but God is always watching and waiting. How, you ask? Think about how Jesus found Zacchaeus. Was it a coincidence that the sycamore tree was there so that a vertically challenged tax collector, hated by a crowd that would never let him pass, could climb and be seen? And was it a coincidence that the same tree provided a platform so that when Jesus called Zacchaeus's name, Zacchaeus was more than front and center: He was up and in view of the One who longed to meet with him? I don't believe in coincidences. God seeks what is lost—always has, always will—and that means He will use anything to reach us if we are willing to trust and believe.

God doesn't stop there. Not only does He *seek* the lost, God also *saves* the lost. This wasn't—and isn't—a game for Jesus. The wee little man in the sycamore tree might make for great Bible songs and rhymes, but for Zacchaeus, and those like him, it isn't a game, either. It means everything. God's goal in drawing close to us through Jesus is not just that we might know our sin, but also that God might transform our lives and make us new in the midst of that sin. Calling Zacchaeus by name was one thing; changing his heart and life . . . well, that was a miracle.

In the Tree with Zacchaeus

This first encounter teaches us that God makes us accountable for the trash in our lives—not to embarrass or shame us, but so that when we experience the life-transforming grace of Christ, we can understand the difference and commit ourselves to a better way. And what do you know? God is not afraid of the junk we drag behind us. He has seen it all before.

Friend, let's stop making excuses for living in the filth. Let's stop thinking of everyone we can blame, and take some responsibility for where our lives have landed. It's trash-bagging time and, believe me, we will not regret it. The sorrow of past mistakes and bad choices needs to be thrown to the curb so that someone much more capable than we can haul it away and give us something new.

Okay, so we might have to climb a tree or two. Why? Because we are there and because we need a glimpse of something better.

We may get a few bruises, scrapes and cuts along the way, but we won't let that stop us. In fact, we'll name them. We'll call them swallowing our pride, letting go of our shame, forgetting our pain, getting out of our own way.

And I have some great news for you: While you are busy naming the things that have held you back, done you in or beaten you down, God will be calling your name. And you will never be the same again. Jesus is coming to your house today!

Grab your trash. Head for the curb. Climb that tree.

Everything looks different up there.

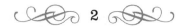

2

The Second Encounter:
The Woman at the Well

JOHN 4:1-42

He who is alone with his sins is utterly alone.
DIETRICH BONHOEFFER, *LIFE TOGETHER*

Most of us say we thirst for God, but do we really?

I have been thirsty many times, but I have never experienced real thirst. A friend of mine who served in Iraq described the difference as a matter of "drops."

"Drops?" I asked.

"Yeah, drops," he said. "You know, like when we say we are thirsty, usually we mean we would like a glass of something, maybe cool water, tea or a soft drink. But, when you experience *thirst* . . ." he continued, "you would take even a few drops of water and consider yourself fortunate."

If we use my friend's standard, does what we call our religious routine translate into a true thirst for God? Or is it more like ordering a glass of tea? Would we take only a few drops if that were all that was offered and be satisfied?

I want to ask you, *What is it that you really want in life?* Or perhaps I should ask it this way: *What is it that you truly thirst after?* After all, we say we *want* many things—more money, a better job, a better house, a better relationship. But, what is it that we crave, need, can't live without? What is it that means so much deep within us that a few drops would suffice if that were all we could find?

The First Mary

Recently on a trip to the Midwest, I met two Marys, and the first one made me think about this whole question of what we can't live without. Mary sat next to me in the airport while I waited for my connecting flight. She was young, probably in her late 20s, and very attractive. She dressed borderline provocative, in a style that ensured people would notice her. She was also a people person.

When she sat next to me, as I ate my turkey on rye, Mary immediately struck up a conversation. She talked about the weather (really!) and then about visiting her aunt in Indiana, the party she had attended the night before, and the new guy she had met who would hopefully become her new "plaything." Throughout the conversation, Mary texted with friends and, if I remember correctly, even answered two calls on her cell phone. It was a long layover. Or at least it felt that way.

I responded to her with the occasional "Yes" or "Sure" and maybe a smile or two as she talked. I always try to be pleasant in these situations, but not overly friendly. Another gentleman sat down on the other side of Mary. He appeared more interested, not necessarily in what she had to say but in Mary herself. She would turn and talk with him for a minute, but she would always move back or turn my way as a means of keeping me in the conversation. I found that courteous, even if I had no desire to be included. I didn't want to be rude, but I have learned from long layovers that it is best to mind your own business. Unfortunately, for me, God doesn't always agree.

After several minutes of the conversation, Mary, with a giggle, said, "I guess I'm just a girl trying to have a little fun in this world." I kept playing with my new iPhone.

The other gentleman said, "I agree. Life's too short not to let your hair down and enjoy a little." My eyes remained fixed on the iPhone.

"You're telling me!" Mary said, laughing. "What do you think?" directing her words to me.

I looked up and responded, "Life's never dull for me. I have three little girls who keep things pretty interesting."

"Three girls? Wow!" Mary said. "Do you have pictures?"

I was suddenly and fully engaged in the conversation. "Sure. Don't all doting fathers?" I pulled out my wallet and showed Mary and the gentleman the many pictures of my three girls. *Did I have pictures?* Ha.

The man, who was obviously not interested in my pictures, interrupted and said to Mary, "Hey, I've got a few minutes before my next flight. Would you like to get a drink?"

Mary, who was still looking at the five or so pictures I had handed her, looked up briefly to say, "No, I think I'll pass." Gone were her giggles and flirty nature. She was genuinely interested in the photos.

The gentleman replied, "You sure? I know a great bar around the corner in the terminal."

Mary never responded. Instead, she looked at me and asked, "What are their names?"

Before I answered, the gentleman gathered his stuff together and moved on.

"Well, that's Sarai Grace," I said, pointing to my oldest. "She is tall for her age."

"She's beautiful!" Mary said.

"Yes," I replied. "She is the spitting image of her mother."

"Your wife must be very pretty."

At that point, I pulled out a picture of my wife. "Here, see for yourself."

"She *is* beautiful," Mary replied. "You are a very lucky man."

"I certainly am," I agreed. "The middle one is Juli Anna," I said, as I pointed to my little redhead.

"She looks more like you, with the blue eyes and all," Mary said.

"Yes, but she *acts* like her mother," I responded. "She is full of life and loves every day."

Mary smiled. "And the little one?" she asked.

"That's Emma Leigh. She's the baby," I said. "She is a mixture of both of them, a blend of their looks and personalities."

"That must have been who you were talking to when I walked up?" Mary asked.

I remembered that I had been on the phone when Mary sat down. I had been consoling my youngest daughter, who had had a hard day at school.

"Yes. She had a bad day at preschool," I said, looking up at Mary. "It seems the teacher wouldn't let them go outside for recess. That didn't sit well with Emma Leigh. She needed a little Daddy Time to help make the day better."

Mary smiled again. However, I noticed that her smile was not the same as it was before—it seemed *quiet* now. She seemed quiet, too.

"You are a good dad," Mary said, her tone softer now.

"I hope so," I replied. "They mean everything to me."

"Your wife is very lucky, too," Mary said.

Feeling a little uncomfortable, I replied, "I am very blessed."

"I hope your girls realize how sweet they have it. My father left us when I was in the fifth grade," Mary said, as she looked down and then back up again. "Come to find out, he had a whole other family that he liked better than ours."

Many people might have been shocked by how matter of factly Mary shared this information. But for years, God has placed people in my path who, for one reason or another, let their guard down and tell their stories. I realize that this is the power of the Holy Spirit and that it is God who uses me for such encounters. That's not to say that I am always ready or willing. As I mentioned earlier, most times I just want to mind my own business, but God usually has other plans.

"Do you have any contact with your father now?" I asked.

"About once a year," Mary replied. "I usually see him on Thanksgiving. My older sister and brother have nothing to do with him, but I keep trying to make a connection. Still, most of the time I feel like just an obligation to him."

"Let me guess . . . he doesn't show much affection or give much affirmation."

Mary looked up. "No, he says 'I love you,' but what I would really like to hear . . ." Mary stopped talking and looked away.

". . . is that he is proud of you," I finished her sentence.

"Yes," Mary said, surprised. "How did you know that?"

I was about to say "Lucky guess," but it wasn't. I had seen my share of Marys during my ministry—young girls forgotten by the fathers who never helped them forge their identities in the world. Usually, these girls grow up to be overachievers but also deeply wounded and broken, chasing after affirmation from wherever they can get it. And, many times, they find themselves in unhealthy relationships that only accentuate the void that should have been filled by their father's respect and love.

"I have a friend who is in your situation," I said. It wasn't a lie—I know numerous women who could echo her story.

"I've always gotten anything I wanted from men," Mary admitted. "Hell, I could have gotten that guy," she pointed to the seat where the gentleman had been sitting, "to crawl on all fours for me."

I smiled. She was right.

"You've always gotten what you wanted except from one man," I said, more softly now, knowing that I was treading into tender territory.

Mary looked back at me. "Yeah," she said. "Can I be honest with you?"

"I think we're already doing that," I said.

"I really wasn't trying to pick you up when I sat down and started talking to you. But I did want you to notice me. It makes me feel better to have men do that." I could tell Mary was really working to get the words out.

"Well, I noticed you. You're very pretty," I said, feeling now that I could say it without the confusion that the same words would have caused earlier.

"Thank you," she said, "but I feel kind of embarrassed now having told you. I don't know why I do that to myself because men notice all right . . ." She got up and began to pace.

"And then you get yourself into bad situations?" I asked.

"You would be surprised," Mary said. I had not told her that I was a minister. She had no idea how many times I had heard this same story. "No offense," she continued, "but most men want one thing." Her smile was gone now. "I'm sure you're different, or at least you appear to be. You didn't seem too interested. When you pulled out pictures of your children, your expression changed, though, and I could tell that I had found *your* weak spot."

I smiled.

"I usually just give them what they want, and . . ." Mary trailed off.

"And they give you what you feel you need?" I suggested, asking the question tentatively.

"Yeah, something like that." Mary sat down in her chair and turned to talk. "What are you, a counselor or something?"

"Something like that," I said, smiling. "I am a Methodist pastor."

"You mean I was flirting with a preacher?!" Mary said with an embarrassed smile. "You should wear a sign or something!"

"You don't know the half of it," I said, now laughing with her.

"Well, that would explain the cold shoulder and disinterest at first," she responded.

I said, "Last time I checked, preachers were human, too. In fact, maybe more human than most at times."

For the next few moments, Mary shared a great deal about her life. She had begun the pattern of bad relationship choices early, getting pregnant and having two abortions by the time she was out of college. She married in college, but ended up having an affair with a former boss. The affair destroyed her marriage and what she called "the only good relationship with a man she really ever had." Recently she had been involved with an older, married man, whose wife had confronted him and who was now in divorce proceedings. All the while, there were occasional hook-ups and countless flirtations that seemed to serve no real purpose at all.

"So, am I just really screwed up?" Mary finally asked.

" 'Screwed up' is a tough phrase," I replied. "But I think you know that this is not the way it should be. I believe God has better things for us—more complete things."

"I just don't know what I want sometimes," she admitted, then shook her head. "No . . . I know I *want* a real, meaningful relationship and a family, not a hook-up or emotional game. Is it fun sometimes? Sure. Does it make my adrenaline flow? You bet. But, in the end, it's all so hollow." Mary looked down again. "I just want something real—like what you have. My dad has probably never pulled out pictures of me before . . ."

She stopped talking. In the silence, I said a prayer: *Okay, God, here is the open door, give me Your words.*

"You know, Mary," I began, "I believe that God placed fathers on this earth to be the reminders of what our heavenly Father has placed and promised in us: that we are special and valuable and loved. Sometimes, dads don't live up to that responsibility and they leave their children wandering a bit . . . well, sometimes, a lot." I stopped and waited for her response. She slowly looked up. "The good news is that the broken bridge between what God has placed inside of you and who you are right now is not beyond repair. Sure, your father let you down, and it's okay for you to say that out loud. The one man who was supposed to give you the confidence and dignity to be a whole woman failed you. And you have spent the rest of your life bartering with other men for that approval. But, they don't—they can't—fill that need in you. Mary, that job belongs to God."

Mary listened and I continued, hoping that my words weren't coming off as a sermon, but as sincerely and personally as I meant them. "Just because there are gaps in the connection between how your life should have been and how your life is doesn't mean that you can't find that wholeness. Mary, I believe that you, that all of us, have been created to be whole. Sure, life has not turned out the way you wanted, but that doesn't mean it can't change. Your heart, your affection, your goals and dreams, your body—those have been created for a beautiful purpose, not for shame, guilt or disappointment."

"So, Reverend," Mary said with a smile, "what do I do?"

"That's a big question," I replied. "But if I were talking to one of *my* daughters, I would probably say to call it what it is with your father: Admit that he has let you down and then forgive him, not for *him* but for *you*. Then move on. I'm not saying forget your dad, but know that you won't find the approval and affection you need in him, or in any other man. Move on to something better."

"You mean God," Mary clarified.

"I mean the One who has loved you and been proud of you since before you were born. And who is still waiting for the *real you* to make your way home."

"And who is the *real me*?" she asked.

"Finding out is part of the joy," I said. "No more games, no more quick fixes—and no more lying to yourself. Mary, you already matter to Someone. And He will help you learn to matter to yourself."

At that moment, my flight was called and I reached to gather my stuff.

"Do you have a card?" Mary asked.

I reached into my briefcase and handed her a business card.

"I would like to let you know how things are going. Would that be okay?" she asked.

"That would be great," I said. "I would like very much to know how you're doing. And, if you ever need to talk, just let me know. Oh, and please know that I will be praying for you." I picked up my briefcase. "I enjoyed meeting you, Mary. Thanks for letting a proud dad brag a bit."

"Hey," Mary said, "I hope you have a safe trip so that you can get back and take care of those girls."

"That's my plan," I said, smiling. "Take care, Mary."

And with that, I made my way to the gate.

Thirst

As Jesus sat down beside the well, He rested. Jesus was thirsty and tired from a long day's journey. Like any traveler, He needed the basics to keep Him strong and healthy. And, so, as many times before, He stopped at a well for a drink. Leaving Jesus, the disciples went ahead to find food and water.

Also at the well was a Samaritan woman. The two words together—"Samaritan" and "woman"—spoke volumes about how and why Jesus, or any religious teacher, should have shunned her. Rabbinic law frowned upon men and women interacting in Jesus' day. But for a *Jewish* man to be seen in the company of a *Samaritan* woman was an abomination.

Samaritans were the offspring of the Assyrian conquerors who had shared relations with women from the 10 northern tribes of Israel. The direct descendants of the northern tribes were no more, but the symbol of the destruction of Assyria's in-

vasion lived on in the Samaritans. They served as a living re-
minder to the Jews of the physical, geographical and religious
domination laid on them and their land for centuries. And as
mixed-race children, Samaritans were an affront to Jewish rules
of purity and clean bloodlines. The Jews and the Samaritans
had a long, unhappy history—a history that neither seemed des-
tined to forget.

The passage in John's Gospel implies that the woman at the
well had other problems, too, apart from her gender and nationality. First, she came to *this* particular well. Certainly there were
wells closer to the town where she lived. But still she came to
this site, remote and set apart from the village. This was a traveler's well, not the place where villagers would have come to
draw their water.

Second, the Scripture tells us that the woman came to the
well at the sixth hour. The Jewish day ran from 6 A.M. to 6 P.M.
The sixth hour would have been exactly noon, one of the
hottest times of the day. Everyone would have known better
than to be at the well at midday; people didn't draw water at
that time—it was too hot and deserted. But maybe that was the
whole point.

Let's think a minute. The woman travels past the bounds of
her village (probably passing other wells on the way) to draw
water, and she does so at the warmest part of the day. I don't
know about you, but to me she sounds like a person who went
out of her way to not encounter others. On most days, I'm sure
the plan would have worked beautifully. But as we see so often
with Jesus, all plans are subject to change.

One other thing . . . we shouldn't miss what the setting and
timeframe say about Jesus. Why did He wait here while His disciples went into town for food? Why was He traveling in the
heat of the day? Was Jesus' weariness just physical, or did He
need a little alone time, too? Hey, these are just questions, but

remember: We've already seen a glimpse in Zacchaeus's story (and there are more to come) of Jesus connecting with an interesting character at an interesting place when He seemed to be on His way somewhere else. This scene at the well reminds us that we are all going somewhere for some reason. And whether they are by a well or in an airport waiting area, our interactions along the way (or desire for no interaction at all) tell us more about where we are headed than any words could.

Consider this: Mary from the airport was flying all right, but not just on airplanes. Her life was a series of layovers, bumpy routes and bad weather. What she really wanted was to land and rest a bit, to find herself and to get the navigation equipment right. The woman at the well? She was thirsty all right, but not just for water. Her life was a series of long, solitary walks past perfectly good wells to draw water in seclusion at the worst part of the day. What she really wanted was a cool drink of acceptance and forgiveness, and to lay down the burden from the heavy buckets of shame and self-doubt she was carrying. Mary's and the Samaritan woman's conditions forced them both to avoid real encounters as often as possible. Real encounters bring self-reflection and evaluation; neither the woman at the well nor Mary thought they were interested. The questions hurt too much, and the consequences might require going places they were unwilling to travel. No, it was safer to walk farther and fly higher.

Here is one of the lies we bridge-broken people believe: *The bridge is out, so I will spend the rest of my life swimming the river with its bad currents and deep water. Maybe that's what I deserve. Maybe that is the only option left.*

It's not true. It's not what God knows and it's not what those who know His heart believe. They know something better is possible for all of us, no matter how far we've gone from who we were meant to be.

Meeting People Where They Are

Over the course of my life, I have looked to Mother Teresa as an example of tenacity, hope and purpose. Was she a saint? I will let the Church debate the specifics of beatification, but, in my eyes, her heart was as faithful and true as any I have seen. Recently in an article published in *Newsweek*, Christopher Hitchens, a self-described atheist and critic of the faith, cast Mother Teresa in a light far different from that of the suffering servant that many of us believe her to have been. He described her as questioning, rigid and often conflicted about her own faith and journey.

The article sent shock waves through the Catholic, and many Protestant, faithful. Hitchens essentially unveiled Mother Teresa—hold on to your hat—*as being human*. I believe both Hitchens and Mother Teresa's defenders miss the point. Because she was human, she questioned; because she loved God, she believed her questions were worth asking.

One thing is certain: If you read the writings of Mother Teresa and examine her example, you cannot help but be amazed at her selfless nature, as reflected both in her personal faith and in her efforts to meet the needs of the world. So what if she had questions? She continued to live like Jesus even while deeply questioning the mysteries of God.

Do I hope that her questions were settled before she died? Certainly. Do I wish her the peace that she craved for the world? Absolutely. Do I still marvel at her example? Unquestionably. Mother Teresa's power came in being the hands and heart of Jesus in the midst of her confusion, not in spite of it. She met people, as Jesus did, where they were along her journey, and she loved them for it.

A friend of mine met Mother Teresa not long before her death and found her to be an incredibly real and humble woman. When my friend asked Mother Teresa why she so openly touched even lepers, AIDS patients and other "untouchables" of the city, her response was straightforward and definite: "Because that is what Jesus would do."

Now, friend, it is easy in our cynical, modern world to dismiss the power of her answer. I can't anymore, and I don't want you to, either. Jesus met people where they were, plain and simple. He touched them, talked with them and cared for them . . . even *became* one of them. Jesus knew human need.

But Jesus did this not only to meet their needs but also to change their lives. The only way to speak real truth and see real change is to begin where people are. Most churches today don't understand this. We wait for people to come to us, dressed neatly, with all their problems worked out, before we accept them. Never mind that none of us has our problems worked out, but as long as you don't tell me about yours, we're okay. In our churches today, protecting perception or image is not just a choice; it is a preference.

Jesus met the Samaritan woman at the well, and He began the conversation about "well" things and about what all thirsty people might discuss. He didn't convey a false bravado or set conditions on what a Samaritan might need to do or not do in order to be in His presence. He simply sat with her and talked.

Let me stop here and do a little preaching! Jesus knows *our* needs, too, and He meets us where we are. We don't have to be good enough, smart enough or religious enough to earn an audience with Him. He simply craves to be present with us. We can walk in, run in, limp in, crawl in or be brought in—it doesn't matter. We don't have to fix ourselves up for this date or get the words just right. No, Jesus waits for us to look up and see that He is here.

The first real lesson we learn from this story is that church and religion do not equal where Jesus is. Of course, we hope God can be found in both, at least I do. But Jesus is more plainly present at out-of-the-way wells and on dusty roads, asking normal questions about your day and your path and your life. Why does He do this? Because *that* is who Jesus is. Not the venerated statue, lauded historical figure or far-off God. On the contrary, He's sitting next to you, wondering if you would like to take a new direction, to find a new way.

For those of you who wonder where God is, don't look much further. God is with you. Immanuel (one of Jesus' names means "God with us") remains the primary means by which God invites us into His presence to change our destinies. And now He is even closer, through the power of the Holy Spirit. So stop thinking that you can run from God's presence. God knows exactly where you are—you've never been that good at Hide and Seek anyway.

And one more thing: In spite of how much you think God is mad at you for whatever you've done or not done, He is still glad to see you.

Finally, a word for those of us in the Body of Christ who keep waiting for the Samaritans to show up at our wells with their stuff straight and their lives in check before we can love them: Not only is this approach ineffective, it's also not Christian. Don't take my word for it, read the Gospel texts. Jesus found little use for the synagogue as a means of reaching those most in need. Instead, He found them in the hills, by the sea, on dusty roads, under the cover of night and beside out-of-the-way wells. Some thought this habit made Him a saint; others condemned Him as a sinner. Regardless, it placed Jesus in the company of those who needed grace the most; those most thirsty for something real and something new; those who were in real need—those like you and me.

Facing the Camera

My wife, Pokey, teaches teachers. She serves on the faculty at a small Baptist college with a strong teacher-education focus.

Pokey says teaching is the one profession that makes all other professions possible. Her goal for her students is twofold. First, she expects passion for the profession. "It must be a calling," she consistently preaches. "No one can significantly impact or survive the classroom, unless you are called to it." Second, she wants her students to realize the difference between *knowledge* and *learning.* "Knowledge," she says, "is a snapshot of time. Learning is a life-changing experience." (This last principle serves my profession well, too. Too often, students, congregants, listeners and seekers are trying to find the *one principle* that can turn their lives around. This works usually until another storm or struggle appears, precipitating the need for a *new* one principle.)

Recently, a student asked my wife how she encourages those in her classes to embrace learning, not just knowledge, and approach their profession with passion. Her answer was simple, in that it had little to do with strategies or skill sets: "I begin by helping my students confront the problems and possibilities of their own journeys."

"What do you mean?" the student asked.

"I start with what you know . . . what you have experienced," Pokey responded. "What do you remember about your school experience? Was it positive or negative? Did it make you want to learn? What about your family? Did your parents read to you as a child?"

"What does that have to do with my being a teacher?" the student interrupted.

"We are all wired up in certain ways, and our experiences have shaped that wiring, leading us to respond and perform at certain levels in certain situations," my wife replied. "And usually, these encounters through our various journeys have determined many of our expectations, boundaries and perceived limitations."

The student's ears perked up. "You mean my life prior to school will impact the kind of teacher I am?"

"Not just the kind of teacher you *are*, but also the way you will view the kind of teacher you can ultimately *become*," Pokey confirmed. "The journey doesn't just affect our present, but also our possibilities. Teaching is about *soul work*. Even if you aren't religious, most people would agree that we are tapestries of various woven experiences that shape us into who we are."

"Like the fact I am from a divorced home?" the student interjected.

"Yes," my wife said. "Let me ask, did you play 'school' as a child?"

"All the time."

"Why?"

"I don't know—I haven't really thought about it."

"During your parents' divorce, was there anyone who stood out as being very supportive?" Pokey inquired.

"Yes . . ." the student's voice trailed off, as though she could see where the questions were going. She finally responded, "There was my second-grade teacher who spent a lot of time with me. I remember her being the one who encouraged me."

"Anything in particular stand out about how she encouraged you?" my wife then asked.

The student thought a minute. "Yes," she said. "She used to tell me that things were going to be all right. That my parents' divorce was not my fault. And . . ." the student's eyes filled with tears.

"And?" Pokey prodded gently.

"That God had a special plan for me, and that one day I would be able to help other little boys and girls who were going through the same thing," the student responded.

"Do you remember who your favorite children were in your make-believe classroom?" my wife asked.

The student looked, tears in her eyes and a smile on her face. "Yes," she said. "The ones going through tough times . . . like divorce."

"I did the same thing as a child," my wife said. "I used to line my dolls up and teach away. However, I would stop occasionally to wipe a runny nose or help with a problem . . ." my wife handed a tissue to the young teacher, "or take care of one of my students having a tough time."

Pokey told me this story over dinner that same evening. "Not all of my students are that reflective or aware of what drives them," she said. "But if they can get to that place, it sure does make the next steps much easier."

My wife and I sat for a minute talking about our own journeys as the children of divorced parents. "People can't confront others without first confronting themselves," she said. "Some lessons actually begin *before* the beginning." We laughed.

You have to know my wife to understand why this conversation was out of sorts for her. She is very fair-minded but tough. Her expectations are high, especially for her students. She believes those who teach are the front lines in the battle for what our children can become. And she earned her stripes as a young teacher, while grinning through the struggles of an often-sick husband and difficult circumstances. She doesn't have much time for whining and underachievement.

But I have also watched her with her students, holding their hands and wiping their tears as they deal with the every-dayness of life. Behind her tough façade is a generous and compassionate heart that wants the best for and from people.

One of the ways she does this is by helping her students go beyond the details of just obtaining a degree to the place where a true career calling is born. My wife loves to watch as the light goes on in her students and they see, some for the first time, the real potential of who they can be. But as my wife says, people can't grasp their potential until they take an honest look at where they are.

Confronting self is probably the most difficult thing we do in this world. It is easy to evaluate others; turning the camera on ourselves is a different story. Several years ago, I began hosting a television program called *Time That Makes the Difference*. It is a 30-minute program that includes a Sunday School lesson and mini-sermon. For years, I had watched the program and had offered my armchair critiques. The work had looked easy, and I had often wondered why the host wouldn't *do this* or *change that*. That was, of course, until I started to host the program myself. I quickly discovered that talking to a TV camera was not as easy as it appears and that a great deal of work and effort goes into every program. I remember sitting motionless in the production room the first time I saw myself on camera, wondering who in the world that person was. Although I have still not gotten used to that feeling, over time I have learned to watch and critique myself without the overwhelming urge to run screaming from the building. Whether it is on camera, before a counselor or looking in the mirror, self-evaluation is tough business.

But in order to move forward with real progress and take hold of a new future, it must be done. From the first taping, I knew this. My wife knows it with her students. And Jesus knew it with the woman at the well.

After He had met her where she was, Jesus helped the woman see herself, maybe for the first time, as she really was. This included unveiling all of her blemishes, but also her potential—you really have to confront the one in order to get to the other. When the woman pressed Jesus about where His bucket was and about His plans to provide this living water of His, Jesus asked her to go get her husband. She didn't have a husband, she said. Jesus pointed out that she had had five of them, and the man she lived with now was not her husband. It went without saying that the life she lived was not healthy. It strikes me that He did this right out in the open, sitting by a well, talking about water. You have to love Jesus; He wasn't afraid of anything or anyone, just as He wasn't afraid of any secret that the woman might hold deep within.

I'll admit that I don't like this part of my job—I'm not fond of pushing people to face their problems and situations. Personally, I would rather sit back and pretend that the world is perfect. The more perfect the world is (or at least the more I believe it is), the less the world needs me to testify and live my faith. Yes, it is a copout, but I want to be honest. As I told you when I recounted my interaction with Mary in the airport, I would rather mind my own business. I used to think this was just out of respect—that I didn't want to get into another person's issues or life. However, I realized later that I preferred this hands-off approach to faith because it was easier on me, not the person in question. Thankfully, God doesn't mind getting into our business. On the contrary, He knows our needs and wants us to face them so that we can move on to find wholeness.

Building back the bridge between what we are and what we are meant to be requires more than just talking about the fact that the bridge is out. It requires that we face our situation head on and then ask, *What can I do to move forward?* and *How can I build again?* Jesus wasn't afraid of pushing people out of their comfort zones because He knew that in all of us something better exists. Sure, the woman at the well had made some bad choices and there were some bad choices made for her, but that wasn't the end of the story. Heck, it wasn't even the *right* story. Jesus revealed the real story in her, and He gave her the option to write a new chapter for a new beginning.

Look at what happens next: The woman leaves the well, goes back to her village and announces, "You've got to come meet this man. He told me everything that I had ever done" (see John

4:29). You have to read between the lines to see the real power of this encounter. Remember, this was a woman who usually went out of her way not to see anyone, even walking to a faraway well in the heat of the day. But, now, after her encounter with Jesus, she runs back to her village and announces a new way. She has a new confidence in her soul that, ultimately, gives her a confidence to reenter her life.

The best gift that God gives us through Christ is a reconnection to the identity that He intended for us from the beginning. Though it is not easy and so many of us resist it because of the discomfort in confronting the disjointed places and feelings of our lives, once we embrace those lessons and confront our situations, we can also see the potential of a new future. A future that does not hold us hostage. A future that frees us to reenter our world and live again.

The Second Mary

Coming home from the same trip on which I met the first Mary, I sat down in my airline seat, prepared for an easy flight. A few minutes later, a small, frail lady took the seat next to me and placed her bag beneath the seat in front of her. As she worked to fasten the seat belt, I asked if I could help. She politely agreed, and I adjusted the belt and put the snaps in place. She thanked me and we prepared to taxi to the runway.

Traffic was heavy for take-off. The pilot announced that we were fifth in line and so there would be a short wait. At that announcement, the lady turned to me and said, "I don't like flying very much."

I put down the magazine I was reading and answered, "Ma'am, I don't much like flying either." I really don't mind flying—after all, it is as safe and easy as any form of travel—but the delays and crowded flights are not enjoyable.

"I only do it in order to visit my son in Indiana," the lady answered. "I live in Louisiana, way out in the woods." Being from the South, I knew that "way out in the woods" meant that she was from the country, probably living in a small, rural community. No, I would imagine that flying was not enjoyable for someone like her.

"How often do you visit your son?" I asked.

"About once a year," she replied. "He moved away many years ago to work with General Motors. He always said that he would move back after a few years, but I didn't believe it." She reached for her bag and pulled out a small wallet. "He met a local girl and they got married a few years after he moved." She pulled out a picture of a middle-aged man, his wife and what looked to be several children and grandchildren. "I knew then that he would never move home. The Bible says a man leaves his mother and father and begins a new family. . . . We wanted him to be happy, but it was certainly difficult to not have him around. That was almost 40 years ago."

I looked at the picture and said, "He has a beautiful family. How many children and grandchildren?"

She smiled. "He has three girls, seven grandchildren and, now, a new great-grandson." She pointed to the young lady in the far left of the picture. "She gave birth two weeks ago. That is why I made the trip to see my son. I certainly had to meet my new great-great-grandchild."

Wow, I thought. My wife's great-grandmother had lived long enough to see the birth of our first child. It was one of the great joys of her life to hold our new daughter in her arms. For a moment, I thought of how generations may change, but the simple joys of life remain the same.

"I am sure you enjoyed your visit," I said.

"Oh, yes," she said. "But I always enjoy going home, too. I don't mind visiting, but Indianapolis is too big for me.

I miss my cats and dogs and recliner."

Now this was language I understood. I, too, missed my favorite chair. But to hear her say it made me feel better for thinking it. "I agree with you," I said, laughing.

"My name is Harriet," the woman said. (Okay, so her name was not Mary. But I had you going for a while.)

I introduced myself, and we shared pleasantries about traveling, soft chairs and children. We had talked for several moments when she said, "Life's funny, isn't it?"

"Ma'am?" I asked.

"Life," she said. "It's funny. I spent most of it wondering what life was like in other places. Now, every time I travel, I just can't wait to get back home." Harriet then looked at me. "Do you travel much?"

"Yes, ma'am," I said. "But when I do, I can't wait to get home, either." This time, I pulled out pictures to show her and told her about my family.

"They are very beautiful. You are a very blessed man," she said.

As she said those words, I thought about my encounter with Mary at the airport before our flight. Almost the same conversation, but from a completely different angle.

"Yes, ma'am," I answered. "I feel very blessed."

"Time is very precious. You shouldn't take it for granted," she offered. "I lost my husband several years ago, but I still miss him like it was yesterday." She looked away for a moment. "He was a very good man. A wonderful provider and father. Now, he wasn't perfect, mind you." She looked at me and smiled. "But he had a way with life."

I loved that phrase. *A way with life*. I thought of Mary and how she seemed to have a way with anything *but* life.

Harriet continued, "My husband always told me that he didn't need anything but me and the kids to be happy. I laughed every time he told me that." A half-smile grew on her face. "I guess I thought it sounded a little, well . . . corny." She was silent for a moment and then said, "I'd give anything to hear him say it now."

As I listened, I realized that age does many things to us, but it doesn't numb the most tender places in our hearts—the places where we love the most deeply. And it doesn't heal some hurts, no matter how much time passes. No matter our age, some feelings never grow old.

"How did you know that your husband was the one?" I asked her.

"Because he knew everything about me and loved me anyway," she said with a grin.

"Oh, I have trouble believing that you were anything but a sweet little lady."

"Maybe now," she said slyly. "But I was quite a siren back in my day. I could cut a rug with the best of them." Imagining this sweet woman, obviously in her late 80s or early 90s, as a young hell-raiser was difficult. But there was a flash of spirit in her eyes that made the thought believable. "However," she said, "the first time I saw my husband, I knew that he was different, and I wanted to spend the rest of my life with him." She touched my forearm and added, "Some things just feel right."

Once again, I thought about Mary. Part of her problem was feeling so empty and lost. Nothing felt *right* to her, and so she spent the better part of her life looking for anything to fill the gap. In Harriet, I found a very different story; she had found her true love and it changed her life forever.

"Do you believe everyone has *someone*?" I asked.

"Yes, I do," Harriet said. "It's just that people are too selfish or impatient for the right one to come along." She paused a minute and then added, "And lazy. Young people want something for nothing. Real love is hard work. It means giving

50/50 . . . no, 100/100 to make it work." Her little voice grew a bit stronger. "I didn't always like my husband. He could be very difficult, but I knew I loved him and that we were committed to each other. And . . ." her voice lowered again as she reflected, "and he believed in me—he believed in *us*."

The wisdom of those words struck me. Their marriage worked because they knew each other, loved each other and believed in each other. It wasn't a complex formula, but it wasn't easy, either. And that was the difference.

For Mary, for the woman at the well and for any of us who wonder if the bridge is too broken: Sometimes, to make it work, you confront the broken bridge, jump back in the raging current and begin building again. As a friend recently reminded me, *If God is God, He is already in the water with you.*

Drawing Water with the Woman at the Well

The lesson of the second encounter is found in how Jesus meets the woman at a point where her problems are reparable. Nothing in His demeanor or words suggests that her life or situation was beyond repair. She thought so, but Jesus knew better. Jesus met her with a straightforward approach. He didn't make her become something she wasn't in order to help her. Jesus never tried to console her in her troubles. And He never condemned her for her bad choices. Instead, Jesus offered her a realistic appraisal of her situation and then provided a solution: the truth.

The Adversary only needs to convince us that the lie is inevitable, or the only option, in order to stop us in our tracks. Mary had almost convinced herself that her life would consist of one broken path after another, that she was doomed to some perpetual pattern of emptiness. The woman at the well believed her thirst could never be filled, except by bad choices, out-of-the-way relationships and less-than-fresh water. Both of them were prepared to be thirsty, thinking that the good life, the living water, had dried up.

But encountering the truth means seeing that our thirst doesn't have to last forever, and there's real power in that. Told correctly and honestly, the truth simply states the facts—it doesn't play favorites, judge or condemn. No, truth tells us, *Okay, so the bridge is out. You can't pass over it this way. But it is also not irreparable. Stop trying to swim the stream. God didn't intend for it to be this way.*

Which brings me back to my second Mary—okay, Harriet.

As our plane landed, she turned and asked, "What do you do for a living?"

By now, you know how I feel about that question. But I responded, "I am a pastor."

"Well, I hope you preach the truth," she said emphatically.

"I try to."

"You know what I would tell people if I were a preacher?" she countered.

"No, ma'am, but I would like to hear it."

"I would tell these young people that life is not a bunch of leaps and bounds, but a series of steps and stumbles. Okay, so you make a few bad choices, or even a lot of them. That doesn't mean the road went anywhere; it just means you left the road." She said this while pointing her finger at the air. "So you know what you do?"

I didn't have time to answer.

"You find the road again and walk back to it and head in the right direction. That's how you have a good marriage. Sure, my husband and I wanted to kick each other in the ditch a time or two," she declared, laughing at her own analogy. "But, we kept grabbing each other's hand, sometimes crying and sometimes laughing . . . but we kept on moving."

My new friend paused a minute and then looked up at me. "Sometimes it was a hard road. We got thirsty and hungry for the wrong things along the way. But we always knew what the real food was and where we could find our strength. We never forgot that, at least not for long. The key was, we didn't make the journey alone."

And so it was with Harriet and her husband, whose days were like all of ours: sometimes hot and dusty, weary and long, but also joyful and memorable and worth it. They learned to draw living water from a good well, together, in the cool of the day, and it never ran dry.

3

The Third Encounter:
The Man with a Demon-
Possessed Son

MARK 9:2-29

We were called to preach his gospel and feed his sheep.
We were, in other words, presented with Jesus himself as our model,
so that most of us could only imagine ourselves
disappointing everyone in our lives
from God on down.

BARBARA BROWN TAYLOR, *LEAVING CHURCH*

I always wondered what it was like to feel utterly alone. My entire life I have had family and friends willing to stand by me through life's storms. As I would meet people who described the anxiety of loneliness, even in a room full of loved ones, I wondered how these feelings could have such a powerful hold on people's lives. After all, why didn't they just *choose to feel better or simply pull themselves together*? I thought this until it happened to me . . .

You may have already guessed that open-heart surgery for hemophiliacs is rare and risky—of course, add HIV and hepatitis-C to hemophilia, and the situation gets even more complicated. My chances for survival depended on the ability of the doctors to control bleeding, in addition to the normal risks associated with the procedure.

It was a Wednesday afternoon when I learned that I would have surgery. Doctors performed a heart catheter on Friday of that week, which provided a picture of a major blockage in the LAD (lower anterior descending) artery. It was one of the big ones. The doctors scurried to cover their bases and scheduled the operating room for the following Monday.

After the heart catheter was installed, my spirits remained high. Friends and family gathered to pray and encourage me, and it felt, in many ways, like any other social gathering. I laughed, prayed and talked with visitors about the procedure, about my endless share of misfortunate circumstances and about having faith. Although slightly anxious, I felt that this Good Friday seemed . . . well, "good," albeit uncertain.

However, on Saturday morning, I awoke to the strangest feeling, unlike anything I had felt before. I felt edgy and fearful. As I went through various tests in the morning, I tried to keep a "business as usual" mindset, but deep down, something was clearly wrong. I knew my children would arrive at the hospital around lunchtime, and I wanted them to have my undivided attention. I was excited about their coming and did not want to miss a single minute—they are beautiful children, lots of fun to be around, and I expected their visit would be the highlight of the day. Nonetheless, I couldn't help but feel a sense of dread.

Just before lunch, I broke out in a cold sweat and my head began to hurt. My heart raced, and I described to a friend a sensation that made me want to take off running as though something was chasing me. It was a fearful feeling, the likes of which I had never experienced before. The nurses could tell something was wrong and called a doctor, who diagnosed the problem as pre-surgery anxiety. They prescribed "feel good" medicine that only made me sleepy, not better. I fidgeted, nervous and unsettled, until my children came.

Yet their presence only heightened the feeling, and after only a short time, my wife, who could see my emotional distress, sent the kids home with their grandparents. I kissed them goodbye and watched them leave; then I put my head in my hands and wept. *This was not the way this afternoon was supposed to go. What was wrong with me? Why did I feel this way? Why had I done this to my children?*

The feeling was more than emotional or intellectual. It hurt physically, as much as any injury I had ever had. And the pain pulsated through everything around me. I told my wife I had never felt so lonely, and everyone I saw only reminded me of the pain of "alone." Anxiety attack? Possibly. But it seemed deeper than that. My wife, who was caring and gracious, consoled me and we agreed that the next day would be better.

And . . . it was. Easter Sunday arrived with the Easter Bunny visiting my children in the hospital room. It was a wonderful time as I watched my children tear into their baskets and attack an assortment of chocolate favorites. This time, their visit was wonderful, even though I occasionally got the sense that something was not right, almost out of place, and that, at any moment, the dread and emptiness of the previous day could return. Thankfully, I felt more prepared this time and held myself together.

Because my wife and I had agreed that our daughters needed to keep a normal routine over the coming days, they weren't coming to the hospital for the surgery. So before they left on that Easter afternoon, I remember drawing each one of them close and whispering in their young ears how proud I was of them and how blessed I felt to be their dad. Only the oldest (age 10 at the time) somewhat comprehended the magnitude of what my words really meant—that "just in case," I wanted them to know how much Daddy loved them.

I held back the tears enough to make the scene bearable until the girls went home, and then I again put my head in my hands and wept. This time, however, I felt more complete, as though I had done what was needed. My children had a good day. They were safe and happy. And they knew no matter what, they had a father who loved them and would always be with them.

I went to bed that night not sure of what had happened the day before—or what would happen over the next few days. I knew we had entered uncharted waters and the surf was rougher than we had ever experienced before. The spiritual currents seemed unsettled, and the best I could do was to batten down and hold on. Sometimes, that is the best any of us can do: hope to land in one piece wherever the waves toss us and try to survive.

Reading this passage in Mark 9:2-29, I felt a kinship with this father who was in uncharted territory, concerned for his sick son yet unable to take care of him. I read the anguish in his voice and felt the knot in his stomach. Like any parent, I had worried about my children before, but the feelings that overwhelmed me that Saturday in the hospital were different. I had a sense of complete loss of control—an almost paralyzing fear. I wondered, *What will become of my children if I can't take care of them? What will become of me if I realize I can't?*

Leading up to the surgery, the more people prayed with me about my health, the more I felt overwhelmed by what the future might hold. Satan found the chink in my armor, my weak flank. I had prepared my entire life to deal with any struggle that *I* might encounter. But now my fears were not for me; they were for my children.

Of course, at the time, I couldn't see the lesson God had for me. My heart was breaking and the possible outcome seemed too much to bear. *Why would God do this, not to me but to them? Doesn't He understand what this would mean?*

Weeks later, I learned that God knew very well what I had felt and understood, more than I had ever imagined: the incredible anguish of handing over a child to an unknown future. When we experience such emotions, we are offered a chance to draw closer to the tender father-heart of God, the heart of Good News for any and all of our circumstances. But in the moment, when the pressure is on, it is very difficult to see the hand of God working around us.

A Fragile Glory

Let me pause and broaden the scene. Just prior to this encounter, Jesus had returned from the mountainside with three of His disciples. While on the mountain, they had experienced nothing short of the magnificent glory of God, in what we call the Transfiguration of Jesus. Scholars have debated the significance of this event, many summarizing it as a mix between divine showmanship and the beginning of Jesus' march to the cross. Regardless, Jesus left the mountain with His eyes fixed on the mission ahead.

Peter, on the other hand, was so impressed that he planned to build three altars (one for each of the figures seen on the mountain) so that he could remember in worship what had taken place. The mountain meant something to those who witnessed the scene unfold. And echoing the sentiments of us all when it comes to mountaintop experiences, they didn't want "the moment" to end.

Nevertheless, Jesus encouraged His three disciples to assimilate what they had seen and move on. He knew that no matter the glory of what they had experienced on the mountain, their work was not there. The solitude of the mountain is never the setting for what matters most in this world. The real work happens in the valley. No, our mountaintop time with God prepares us to meet the needs that are farthest removed from the quiet of our devotional lives.

So it is that upon returning to the valley, Jesus encounters a crowd in the midst of a difficult discussion with the religious leaders about healing. Jesus, whom they had thought was still away on the mountain, finds an excited, welcome response when the people realize He is among them.

It is here that Jesus first meets the father with the demon-possessed son. The father had brought his son to the disciples for healing, but the disciples were unsuccessful. Frustration had then led the father to the scribes and religious teachers, who seized on the situation as a way of casting doubt not only on the disciples' abilities, but on those of their Master as well. What an amazing scene! Here are Jesus and three disciples, who have just experienced one of the most important displays of divine power recorded in Scripture, surrounded by a desperate father with his sick son, the rest of the (seemingly powerless) disciples, the plotting religious leaders and a questioning crowd.

It reminds me of returning from a spiritual life retreat or really great church conference only to have others steal my joy with the "cares of this world." I wonder if Jesus rolled His eyes (I do!) or rubbed his forehead, wondering, *Why did I come back again?* His frustration at the situation is evident and unmistakable: "You faithless generation! How long am I to put up with you?" (see Mark 9:19, *RSV*).

The first time I read this passage, I missed the importance of Jesus' reaction. When I realized what Jesus had said, I remember sitting back in my chair thinking, *Did Jesus just say* that? *Did I just hear The Tone?* You know what I mean by The Tone, right? Like when your mom or dad would, in complete exasperation, look at you and say, "What am I supposed to do with you?" Make no mistake; that's the same Tone Jesus used here. Call it a Calgon moment if you like, but no matter how you read it, Jesus wanted to go back to the mountain. Who wouldn't?

Some scholars may argue that Jesus knew the questions before the religious leaders asked and that the situation only served as a convenient occasion for Him to display God's wisdom and power. But if we read the Gospels closely, it becomes clear that

God unveils His power through the fragile humanity of Jesus. From being born in a stable to His temptation in the wilderness, the Jesus who looks and feels like you and me provides the most profound glimpse into the nature of God's redeeming love. I believe the situation with the demon-possessed son points in a different direction, away from a demonstration of divine power and toward something else.

Jesus is obviously frustrated with the continued lack of understanding from those around Him—and for the first time in Scripture, we see Jesus openly question whether or not those whom He has chosen can actually follow Him. As Jesus stands amid the doubts of the scribes, the confusion of the disciples and the despair of the father, it seems clear to me that He can't help but think how far the mountaintop feels from this place. There, the powerful hand of the Father had been unveiled, but standing here in the midst of such confusion, considering both this situation and the future ahead, those mountaintop moments of transcendence seem like such a fragile glory.

Of all of the encounters explored in this book, this may be the most poignant, because it is the only time when Jesus seems to feel the ache of God's absence, too. Not that God has completely disappeared—not yet, anyway (see Mark 15:34). But in His humanity, Jesus clearly feels the frustration and loneliness that invade us all when we experience the presence of God and then come down from the mountain. As Jesus turns to address the concerns of the waiting father, we can't help but notice that Jesus has His own concerns and that His distress, whether or not it fits neatly into our theologies, tells us more about Christ than several mountaintops put together.

Added to His anxiety was the pitiable sight of this father, who cared for little else beyond relieving his son's suffering. He was simply a dad trying to find someone—anyone—to help his child. The father probably had turned to one healer, magician or religious leader after another, only to be disappointed by the results. Then he had heard of Jesus' disciples . . . but even they couldn't cast out the demon.

Finally he lands in the middle of this crowd, at the center of a debate much deeper than his situation—all the while searching for someone to help his child.

Turning a Child Away

I met Jimmy Allen in the spring of 1999 at a conference for HIV/AIDS in Jackson, Mississippi. I worked as a volunteer for the organizing committee and it was my job to assist Rev. Allen, who was a speaker for the conference, during his stay.

Though this was our first encounter, I had heard bits and pieces of his story for several years. Rev. Allen was a two-term president of the Southern Baptist Convention during years when the denomination was more moderate doctrinally and politically. He had pastored First Baptist Church of San Antonio, a large, growing congregation viewed by many as a flagship church for the Baptists.

Rev. Allen had provided leadership as the denomination struggled with difficult issues, most notably the Civil Rights movement and the battle over biblical inerrancy. But nothing could prepare him for how his life and ministry would change in the early 1980s, when his son informed him that his daughter-in-law, Lydia, while pregnant with her first child, had contracted HIV through a blood transfusion. Following the birth of Rev. Allen's second grandchild, the family discovered not only Lydia's positive HIV status, but that both children also tested positive. Bryan, the infant, died in 1986. Lydia died in 1992. Matthew, his oldest grandson, lived until the age of 13.

The disease devastated the family, but it was the Church that broke their hearts. After Rev. Allen's son Scott learned about his wife's condition, he immediately shared the news with the senior pastor of the congregation in Colorado where he served as an associate pastor. The church fired Scott the next day. Over the next months, after relocating to Dallas, the family struggled to find childcare, schools or even a church home, because fears about the disease caused people to keep the Allens at arm's length.

Scott, while reeling from the loss of his family, one member at a time, grew disillusioned over the next months and years, not only with the Church but with the Christian faith in general. He was convinced, as he told his father, that the Church was "just like any other business." Today Scott practices Taoism, having left Christianity altogether.

Rev. Allen shared his story with me as we moved from one event to another at the HIV/AIDS conference. I sat stunned—not at the devastation of the disease, for I understood the natural progression of the virus and its effect on the body—but even after everything I had experienced in my own journey as an HIV-positive Christian, I found it difficult to grasp the Allen family's abandonment by the Church.

"What have we become?" I remember asking Rev. Allen.

"It's not that we have become *anything*," he said sadly. "It's that we have become *nothing* to so many."

At that point, Rev. Allen told me about the final days of his grandson Matthew. He visited Matthew every week, especially during the final months of his life. Rev. Allen often asked what Matthew wanted to do, and the two of them would take off on some adventure. In Matthew's final days, the adventures grew difficult as his health failed.

During one of their final visits, Matthew, covered with tubes and confined to a wheelchair, asked his grandfather to take him to McDonalds. Matthew always liked McDonalds, but to Rev. Allen, it seemed an odd place for a dying little boy's final adventure. But as good grandfathers do, he packed Matthew up and off they went to the golden arches. When they arrived, Matthew asked his grandfather to take him out to the playground. He was not eating much those days anyway and, as Rev. Allen soon discovered, food was not the reason for his visit.

When he wheeled his grandson through the playground doors, several kids made their way over to say hello. Matthew laughed and talked like any little boy. As Rev. Allen watched Matthew with the other children, he realized the reason for his grandson's last request: Matthew had chosen McDonalds because he wanted to *belong*, and the children at McDonalds—unlike at church or school—didn't care about his disease, feeding tube or wheelchair. At the McDonalds playground, all little boys are equal.

Rev. Allen finished the story and we drove in silence for several minutes. Both of us, men of the Church who had seen our share of battles over this issue, still found the Church's actions (or lack thereof) difficult to comprehend. And in the years since, I have experienced that awkward and sad silence many times—over different issues, but for the same reason: the inability of the Body of Christ to *act like it*.

"I guess I couldn't imagine a sadder experience in my entire life," Rev. Allen finally whispered. "Of all the places my grandson could have chosen to go during one of his final outings, he did not . . . he *could not* . . . choose the Church." He looked into my eyes and continued, "He couldn't, because when they had a chance, the Church didn't choose him."

I couldn't help but wonder what Christ would have thought of Matthew Allen's final request. After pondering it for a moment, I concluded that Jesus would have driven Matthew to McDonalds Himself and had a ball with him and the other kids, all the while thinking about His wrong-headed, misguided followers: *You faithless generation . . . how long must I put up with you?*

Where Do You Start?

While some people may not like a reading of Scripture that exposes Jesus' more vulnerable side—*What do we do with a Jesus who responds, well . . . like us?*—I like this Jesus. I find comfort in the humanity we see exhibited along His journey. It speaks not only to what God came to accomplish through His Son, but also to the heart of who God is: a God who is not afraid to deal directly—*personally*—with the innermost struggles of heart and soul in each of us.

Think about it for a minute. Haven't *you* grown frustrated at the continued disbelief or uncaring reactions of this world? Haven't *you* tired of watching friends make the same mistakes over and over again? Haven't *you* grown weary in well-doing when the well-doing doesn't seem to make much of a difference? Certainly, you have—and so have I. And if Jesus had not felt these same feelings, God couldn't understand the intense struggle it is for us to try to live like He does. Watching a Jesus who even for a moment feels the desolation of God's distance reassures me in my own emptiness when God cannot be found. Why? Because not only does Jesus understand my pain, He chooses a road through His own anguish that I can walk, too. In essence, because Jesus knows full well the problem, I can trust His solution all the more.

The frustration of Jesus affirms the nature of God's love and intentions for us. We are not some behaviorist experiment. No, we have free will to choose and feel whatever we like. God doesn't want robots. God wants us to choose to love Him freely. But the underbelly of that freedom means a world that must risk living imperfectly, a world that is fragile. So for Christ to be like us means that He must confront this underbelly of imperfection firsthand. Does He sin? No. Does it make Him less divine? Absolutely not! But it does make Him more personal and more aware of our struggles. And it shows us the great lengths to which the God of this universe will go to reach us.

We have a God who understands. As an HIV-positive Christian, it often frustrates me when good and well-meaning brothers and sisters make proclamations about the HIV pandemic with little sense of what the issues really are, how difficult the disease can be and how living with the disease affects not only one's medical condition but the entire scope of one's life. Of course, I am not saying that I want to talk with only those who are HIV positive, but there is something to be said for empathy and actually knowing firsthand the circumstances I live in each day. Counsel from someone who has been touched personally by the disease makes my ears perk up more quickly and the advice is easier to swallow.

In the same way, knowing that my God understands the ins and outs of this world from my perspective makes me love Him even more. I certainly don't want a God who makes the same mistakes I do, but I trust His guidance and counsel because He has taken the time to understand my condition and to do something about it.

What's more, the fact that Jesus understands how circumstances can overwhelm us gives me courage. I don't know about you, but the Adversary loves to distract me from the present and get me thinking about tomorrow. What a wonderful and effective strategy! Satan knows that we have little impact on tomorrow, so he encourages us to think about our situation with a sense of impending loss of control. And if we think about that inevitable loss long enough, it can create a spiritual panic that resonates throughout the whole of our lives. Scripture tells us that Satan comes to devour us like a lion, but I have actually found that Satan is somewhat slothful and prefers to expend as little energy as possible. Why put forth the effort to destroy when, through encouraging our worry and spiritual paralysis, he can help us to destroy ourselves?

Unfortunately, anxiety over tomorrow's needs is not only a tool used against individuals—Satan loves to use it to disrupt the whole of the Church as well. The Body often responds the same way individuals do, only on a larger scale. What else could cause a church to turn away a child based on his or her HIV status, or fire a father at the most critical time of his life (remember the Allens)? Worry, paralysis, distraction . . . *tomorrow*.

While Jesus was on the mountaintop experiencing God's glory with His closest friends, Satan was busy messing in the everydayness of people's emotions, frustrations and fears. When Jesus came back down into the valley, He found a fight for fragile souls raging. Notice how the battle didn't seem terribly critical to those already in it, but Jesus recognized its significance right away: This wasn't just another fight, this was *the* fight—the collision of trust in God and the anxiety the Adversary so desperately wants to create.

What frustrated Jesus when He returned from the mountaintop was not that the disciples couldn't heal the boy; it was that they couldn't grasp *why* they couldn't heal him: disconnection from God (see v. 29). His disappointment is echoed each time we experience disillusionment with circumstances or relationships. Yet His response demonstrates how God steps in to remedy the situation: knowing our condition, understanding our struggle, seeing our imperfections and providing a way to progress. He doesn't just understand our struggle; He has felt it firsthand. God, in the Incarnation, made our fight His fight to the very core of His being.

Sure . . . like you, I prefer the "grand wave" view of God—the God who simply speaks or motions and things happen. But that doesn't work in a world with free will; nor does it allow us to participate in building our lives or the lives of others for the Kingdom. God's becoming like us solves the cosmic dilemma! In the Incarnation, with all of its frail and risky confines, Christ not only provides the means by which we are redeemed, but He also teaches the redeemed how to live faithfully in the world.

As I read the Gospels, they remind me that Jesus couldn't do everything—not because He didn't have the power or inclination, but because the Incarnation placed limits on Him. (Remember, Jesus didn't start walking through doors or appearing mysteriously until after the Resurrection.) Jesus played by the rules of being human; God confined the power of the divine to the nature of humanity.

But although Jesus couldn't do everything—make the disciples get it, help all those who were sick, open the eyes of the Jewish leaders—*He did something.* And that is the lesson for us.

As Jesus confronts the situation with the crowd, His first reaction is very human. He feels the need to make people "understand." He grows frustrated over the religious leaders' taunting and arguments, and the disciples' lack of faith saddens Him. Jesus wants to do *everything. Everything* is a source of great anxiety in our world. We believe that we must say yes to everything, that we must be all things to everyone and that we must provide answers for every question. No demand could be more pressing in our society, or more unattainable. Jesus feels this human desire raising its head, and He does what we all do: He grows frustrated.

But watch His response closely. Jesus knows He can't do everything for everyone, but He chooses to do *something.* He tells them, "Bring the boy to me" (Mark 9:19). *I can't change you—*thinking of the religious leaders—*or ensure you will understand it tomorrow—*looking at the disciples—*but I can do this now.*

By His own design, Jesus couldn't do everything, but He could do *something.* He saw the situation, felt the frustration, and then started with the one thing He could do.

And so, the father brings the boy before Jesus.

Let me ask you a few questions: Where do you start when facing the struggles of this world? Where do you begin when confronted with frustration? How do you cope with imperfection in and around you? How do you live faithfully today when tomorrow is so uncertain and looks so bleak?

How do we begin any significant journey? *One step at a time.* How do we love the whole world? *One person at a time.* How do we confront the uncertainties of tomorrow? *One hope at a time.* Because taking on tomorrow's problems today will always lead to despair.

Yes, He knows our shortcomings, for He was willingly bound by the same limitations. He doesn't expect us to do everything. But can't we start with *something*?

Help My Unbelief

Several weeks following my heart surgery, I realized the full extent of my pre-procedure anxiety when my middle daughter asked if I had been scared of dying.

"I was a little nervous," I said, trying to be a strong daddy.

"You looked real nervous when I saw you in the hospital," my daughter responded. I realized I was caught.

"Well, maybe I was more than a *little* nervous," I said with a wry smile. "Daddy was . . ." I paused for a moment because a small lump was developing in my throat. I had not thought about those emotions in weeks.

My daughter interjected, "Don't you know, Daddy, that when you die, you go to heaven? You don't hurt in heaven. People don't have surgeries, and you don't take medicine either. Why would you be scared of going to heaven?" she asked.

I realized that life and death for my daughter were a neat package of *before* and *after* theology. She understood life from her faith's point of view, and as I sat listening to her, I remembered feeling that way, too . . . once.

But having children changed what I worried about. I had not realized how much until the extreme anxiety I experienced before surgery. My questions for God were not about me any longer, but about my children. My own fate was one thing, but I had rigid boundaries around my hopes for their fate, boundaries that I preferred not to be crossed. It had been a painful and vulnerable time in my life—and I still felt the reverberations.

Yet now my daughter needed an answer. *Who could be scared of going to heaven?*

Regaining my composure, I said, "Daddy was nervous because I didn't want to leave you or your mommy or your sisters. I knew that I would be okay, but I am not the most important thing to me anymore. When you guys came along, all of that changed for me." I looked directly into her eyes. "You became the most important thing to me, and when I was faced with the possibility of not being able to take care of you, that scared me."

I realized the conversation was deep for a seven-year-old. I stopped talking and watched for her response.

Finally she asked, "Daddy, do you love God more than me?"

"Yes," I answered. "I love you so much because I love God more."

"Does God love me more than you love me?"

"Yes. As much as I love you, Juli Anna, God loves you more."

"Well, if you love me and take such good care of me, and if God loves me more, won't He take just as good care of me?"

"Yes, sweetheart, I guess He would," I said, realizing that I had been spiritually bested by my seven-year-old.

"Daddy, you always tell us that when we are scared, that means a part of us doesn't trust God. Do you trust God to take care of us, Daddy?"

"I do trust God, baby," I said with a tear in my eye. "It's just sometimes even Daddy needs help believing it."

I will never forget what happened next. My seven-year-old daughter took my hand and said a prayer *for me*, and I felt for the first time the beautiful truth that this child, so dear to me on Earth as my daughter, was even sweeter to me as a sister in Christ. I had never characterized my relationship with my children in such a way before, but after this moment, I understood the distinction Jesus draws between the deeper connection we have with one another in God—greater even than our family ties (see Luke 8:19-21).

I'm not the only father who has ever been a bit short on faith. As the father of the demon-possessed son brings his son before Jesus, his faith is nearly gone. When Jesus asks how long the affliction had held the boy in its grasp, the father responds, "Since childhood" (Mark 9:21). Then he adds, "If you can do anything, take pity on us, and help us" (Mark 9:22).

When we first read this statement by the father, most of us replay "*If* you can . . ." over and over. *Doesn't this man know who Jesus is?* we think. Of course he does. But he is not just another person seeking Jesus' help. No, he approaches Jesus as the father of a sick child. He wants to believe, but it's not his fate that hangs in the balance. The possibility that he might not be able to take care of his son scares him. How can he trust someone else to do what he cannot?

"If I can?" Jesus replies. "Don't you know that all things are possible for those who believe?" (see Mark 9:23).

The father of the sick child responds immediately: "I do believe; help me overcome my unbelief" (Mark 9:24).

For years, I did not understand the paradox of this answer. How can one believe and yet *not* believe at the same time? It seemed a contradiction until I became a father. Now, however, it is clear to me that the father believes as well as anyone else might believe—after all, he is here asking for help, right? He knows Jesus' reputation and understands the power of His ministry. But in this moment, he also knows that in the deepest places of his heart, he fears that Jesus cannot do what He says He can do. There is just enough distance between the belief in his mind and the belief in his heart to create a place where doubts linger and anxiety rises. The father's fear betrays his lack of trust.

Isn't it ironic how Satan only needs a small chink in our armor to find a way to get at us? You see, the son is not the only one paralyzed in this passage. The emotional and physical strain of the son's illness has caused the father to lose not his faith, but his *assurance* in faith. As a man, he believes in God; as a father, he struggles to trust. His doubt is not spiritual rebellion. On the contrary, the burden for his child outweighs the grasp of the faith he so dearly wants.

Don't judge him. What he is experiencing has happened to all of us who confront the weak link in our spiritual chain. The father's spiritual weakness is his son; mine was the safety and future of my children. What's yours?

After my daughter questioned my understanding of faith, I understood the monumental difference between knowing God and wholehearted trust in Him. We can only know Christ when we are willing to set aside everything—every good, bad, joy, sorrow, laughter, tear, treasure or trial—and to confront our deepest (and loneliest) places that we find on our way to real faith. Yet Jesus doesn't hold it against us that we have difficulty setting these things aside—He understands these emotions because He has experienced the limitations of our humanity.

The father of the sick child pleads that Jesus might not only heal his son, but—greater still—heal his own doubt. I wrestled with doubt as my small but wise daughter painted a picture of heaven and asked me to take a long look at what I knew to be true. And many of you, each day, by your cries or by your silence, testify to the incredible difficulty of wholehearted trust. We "show up," we try to be strong, we say the right words, sing the right songs, even say the right prayers, but do we confront the real issue: that we cannot solve our crisis of faith alone? In this, the father of the demon-possessed son is more honest than most.

In that moment of unbelief, he thinks, *I am his father. No matter my doubts, I must believe that there is an answer. Jesus must do the rest.*

As one who has also looked over the gulf between fearful doubt and confident trust, I have found that, too often, it is not what we believe that is the problem; no, it is the nagging unbelief that lingers in the dark corners of our very human hearts.

He Stood Up

Not long ago, doctors amputated my wife's grandmother's foot due to complications resulting from diabetes. "Nanny" was 81 at the time, so we worried not only about her body's ability to withstand the procedure, but also the emotional strain she would experience. After several years of extreme pain while doctors tried to save her foot, we knew the finality this procedure symbolized. Doctors believed amputation was the best option, but even so, it was not an easy choice.

The surgery was a success. The doctors and nurses provided excellent care. Still, we wondered, when it came time for rehabilitation, how Nanny would ever return to a normal routine. After all, she was 81 and had been through so much—who could predict the outcome?

But "giving up" is not in Nanny's vocabulary. She attacked rehab with a tenacious spirit and made an immediate impression not only on the therapists but on the other patients as well. They were amazed by her iron will that drove her to regain her life and normality. Sure, she had lost a foot . . . but she had not lost her spirit or her desire to truly live.

Nanny moved through the inpatient rehabilitation process more quickly than expected. Following her discharge from the hospital, she began an outpatient therapy routine that included not only occupational guidance but also strength training. For any amputee, but especially for an 81-year-old, the exercises were difficult and tiring. But each day, she improved; eventually she was able to use her walker and accomplish most household tasks alone. In fact, her progress accelerated at such an amazing rate that doctors moved up her prosthesis-fitting date. All of this took place under the gaze of other amputees, so Nanny's story of rehab became an inspiration to others.

One day, while speaking with Nanny's physical therapist, I mentioned our surprise at her pace, strength and mental attitude. I congratulated the therapist for her skillful work with Nanny. "She couldn't have done this without you," I said.

The therapist, with a shy smile, replied, "I'm not so sure about that. She is a remarkable woman."

"I think you are being too modest."

"Not modest, just realistic," she responded. "Our job is not to do the work for them, because we know that people with challenges like these will have to go home and live on their own. They don't need another nurse; they need a chance. It's like this: We may provide the lift, but they have to want to stand."

Her words impressed me—she had assessed her job wisely. Any therapist, whether physical, occupational or relational, provides only the open door or helping hand. It is the willingness of the person to *stand* or *move forward* or *begin again* that ultimately decides the outcome. It was true—many people supported Nanny, but *she* had to "stand up" in order to heal.

And so it was with the healing of the demon-possessed boy. Jesus rebuked the demons and they left the child. He walked over and took the boy by the hand, lifting him from the ground. And then, Scripture states clearly, the child *stood up* under his own strength (see v. 27).

I've often missed the full implication of this last interaction with the boy. Like other bystanders at the scene, I've been consumed with watching the crowd, the disciples or the father instead of observing how Jesus interacts with the child. Before now, the boy has seemed an almost secondary figure to the disciples' confusion, the father's doubt and Jesus' frustration. In fact, we might feel as though the healing of the child is a subplot within the overall story. That is, until Jesus touches the boy. With a calm resolve and caring touch, Jesus responds to the fears of the crowd that the boy might already be dead. His touch, coaxing the boy to his feet, is important. What might easily be overlooked is a significant bond between Jesus and the newly healed child.

I wonder what was going on in Jesus' mind as He helped the child stand. Was He still frustrated at the scoffing of the religious leaders and the confusion of the disciples? I think not. No, in touching the child, Jesus reminded the onlookers and maybe even Himself what the Good News promises. In an encounter filled with failure, doubt and frustration, a standing boy brings the message back to center stage and reminds those watching why Jesus' ministry means so much to so many.

The healing of the boy teaches valuable lessons about living our faith in the midst of life's confusing distractions. And the ultimate point is that our struggles with feeling God's absence—that we are *too far gone* or have *gone too far* to find Him again—result from the world's tendency to encircle us with one storm or another, or even to launch the storm from deep within. Look at what I mean: This episode began with a father needing his son to be healed. What transpired was a series of interactions that did little but distract from the actual purpose. And make no mistake—everyone was affected, including Jesus. Sound familiar? How many times have the routines and bumps of life kept us from the real task at hand?

As the action moves inside the house, the disciples ask Jesus why they couldn't heal the boy. After all, the disciples had healed and performed miracles such as this before (see Mark 3). What was different this time?

Jesus responds, "This kind [of demon] can come out only by prayer" (v. 29). I don't believe He is talking here only about the demon within the boy. No, "this kind" is any force that keeps a person or group of people from seeing and doing the work of God before them. Such demons come in many forms. Could it be the demon of doubt plaguing our thoughts, the demon of frustration veiling our joy, or the demon of anger preventing us from seeing the Messiah in our midst? Of course! And the way to deal with those kinds of demons is through *prayer*.

By "prayer," Jesus is referring to the disciples' relationship with God. The deeper our prayer life, the closer we are to Him. Quite simply, Jesus tells the disciples that they couldn't rid the child of his demon because they had moved away from God. In essence, they had rearranged their spiritual proximity and that had made all the difference. Why? Because even though they had been given the gift once, there was no guarantee that it would continue unless they remained close to the Father.

Jesus wasn't condemning the disciples—He was reminding them that the power of God works only if the conduit is open. As in every other aspect of our relationship with God, He does not force His will upon us. No, there comes a point that, even if after feeling His touch once, we must choose to receive and respond again. Remember that, in the end, even the boy must choose to *stand up* with Jesus.

Do you remember the Sunday School picture of Jesus standing at the door, knocking? A friend of mine provides a new take on this much beloved scene. He insists that Jesus is not asking if He can come inside as much as He is *asking us to come outside* with Him.

Friend, it's time to get rid of your demon, whatever that may be, and stand up with God. Trust me, God is more than aware of your doubt and frustration; He knows the deepest and darkest places of your soul. He knew the doubts harbored by the father of the sick child and, time and again, we see a glimpse of Christ's own struggles.

Satan wants you to believe that any feeling of uncertainty is wrong or somehow blasphemous. What a lie! Remember, Satan's best tool is not to overtly attack our lives. No, his greatest weapon is when he convinces us that we can't be honest with God—no matter that God already knows the core of our self-deception. Unfortunately, many times, we would rather believe the lie than face the weakest link—our greatest fear.

Believing with the Man with a Demon-Possessed Son

What incredible courage the father had in admitting that he didn't know how to shed his doubt and unbelief. After all, no one could have been more in need or have had a greater desire to give the right answer than he. But what did the father do? He didn't just give the *right* answer; he chose to give the *honest* answer: "I do believe, help me overcome my unbelief!" (see Mark 9:24). Most of us in a similar situation would tell Jesus what we think He wants to hear, or at least the "most spiritual" thing we could think to say. Yet this father spoke from his heart. He had nothing to prove and everything to lose . . . his son.

Jesus did what the father asked because God doesn't play games with us. He knows how complicated and bewildering this mixed-up world can be. Remember the focus of this encounter: Jesus knows the limitations of our lives and understands the foundations of our fears firsthand.

Knowing this, friend, take heart—your doubts and fears are not enough to make God turn away. Christ walked the journey too and was burdened by the same imperfections of this world. Capernaum, Bethany, Gethsemane, Calvary—these are more than touchstone locations of Christian heritage; they are the places where God felt His humanity and experienced the sting of our world. And yet, these are also the places where Christ chose to move forward and close the distance between God and us. He did *something* amazing!

This encounter comforts me because I realize that God knew very well the feelings of that father. God, too, had everything to lose—His Son—but He chose to do just that for you and for me. He did so because God knows the other side of our limitations—the potential in us that we cannot see—and His Son ensures that our imperfections don't define us in the end. No, we are defined by how we face our greatest fears and by how we trust the God who stood up for us.

4

The Fourth Encounter:
The Woman Caught in Adultery

JOHN 8:1-11

*We only have to name it, and heed the call of justice
that still waits for an answer.
Like the nameless slave poets who wrote the spirituals, we must
look our brutal history in the eye and still find a way to
transcend that history together.
I am standing here until the Lord takes me somewhere else,
because blood done sign my name.*

TIMOTHY B. TYSON, *BLOOD DONE SIGN MY NAME*

I've been throwing rocks my whole life. As a child, we played a game by a local creek that involved finding stones and then skipping them along the surface of the water. The winner was the one who skipped his rock the most times down the longest stretch of the creek. It was just a game, so long as the stones were thrown away from you . . .

A Dirty Place

Several readings into the first verses of John 8, it occurred to me that the woman brought before Jesus literally landed at His feet. We often move quickly to the rest of this story—the woman's actions and what she was accused of—without taking notice of the scene itself. Here is Jesus kneeling, or sitting maybe, in the Temple square while this woman, probably not looking her best, is thrown or pushed by angry men to the ground at His feet. The place is dusty, hot and dirty. Others gather around just in time to hear those who have brought the woman to Jesus declare her crime—adultery—and the punishment—death.

Push the pause button and hold this image in your mind. This is important. You have the angry accusers, the woman and Jesus. Oh yes, and you have those who have gathered, though even they can't really tell you why. That is the nature of angry mobs. We gather because the action intrigues and distracts us. But who are we kidding? We also gather because something deeply broken inside of us likes it—unless you are the woman on her knees, her face in the dirt at the feet of Jesus.

And that is the missing part of the story—the woman, how she felt and what had brought her to this place. Read from her point of view, this is a painful passage. Her hopelessness is as obvious as the dirt on her face, and there appears to be little that Jesus can do. She is caught in a riptide and is barely holding on. This is nothing short of a rescue mission—there is no other way to describe it. Maybe that is the reason so many of us have read this passage half-heartedly, focusing on the woman's sin or the "gotcha" encounter between Jesus and the religious leaders. These are important, yes, but there is much more here—too much for us, perhaps. The woman's helplessness feels familiar, and as we watch her story unfold, we realize that this is a story about us, about the neighbors we have known and about the many times we have forgotten one another in order to save ourselves.

A Girl Named Sophie

I once knew a girl who changed the way I view this particular passage of Scripture. We'll call her Sophie. The youngest child in a family of five, Sophie was pretty but disheveled both in her appearance and in her soul. Her family came from the wrong side of the tracks—literally, and in the way they lived, acted and treated each other—and they never could seem to work their way back across to the other side. Sophie's mother, though nice enough, spent most of her time working nights at a local factory. Her father was a drunk and spent very little time working at all. The only energy he exhibited was in picking up a bottle or taking a shot at one of his children. For years, rumors of child abuse ran through the community, only to be swept under one dirty rug after another. No one could prove anything and the mother and children would never tell. I suppose their motto was "Dance with the one who brung you"—though the dance seemed terribly violent at times, or at least the bruises pointed in that direction.

Sophie's life at school was no better. In elementary and junior high, she rarely arrived without looking as though she had walked miles to school. She smelled—the result of no one helping her with the hygiene needed for young girls—and she wore mostly hand-me-downs from a neighbor or whatever her mother found at local garage sales. Sadly, on several occasions, Sophie arrived at school only to encounter the sneers and giggles of kids who recognized *their* clothes on Sophie's body. As young children do, her schoolmates made fun of Sophie, and she felt the sting of their jeers. Little girls have it especially tough in situations like this—the pack identifies the weakest outcasts and then viciously attacks. Sophie never had a chance. During these young years, she carried too much into the fight and never knew how to get her fists up.

As I said earlier, Sophie was not unattractive, just forgotten. She had a sweet smile and beautiful green eyes that shimmered when you took the time to look at them long enough. Her body developed early, and by the sixth grade, the boys began to take notice. This only angered the other girls more and made Sophie a target for their continued torture.

The truth is, Sophie grew up without choices. She had no one at home to help her know who she was or what she could be. She had no friends to give her advice or comfort. And, most importantly, no one gave her the positive attention that all people need in order to develop a healthy self-esteem. You know what I'm talking about—the kind of attention our souls crave, the kind that feeds our souls and helps us to believe we are worth something. And if we are starved for the right kind of attention, we will gladly take the wrong kind. Attention, even when it comes from the wrong people for the wrong reasons, is still attention.

As Sophie matured and the boys noticed, she found herself in more and more compromising situations. First, it was the neighbor's son, a junior in high school, who convinced Sophie, then in fifth grade, to perform a sexual act with him. She didn't like it, but the boy said things to her that no one else ever had—and even though he didn't mean them, she liked the lies better than the truth. She lost her virginity the summer between sixth and seventh grade to a friend of her brother's. The event took place in the laundry room of her own house while her father slept off a drunken stupor on the sofa in the next room. By the end of her ninth-grade year, she was more experienced than even girls much older.

Sophie's first pregnancy happened at 15. So did her first abortion, paid for by the boy, who happened to be a star athlete from a neighboring high school. Her second pregnancy came a year later, followed by a second abortion—this one rumored to be the result of a relationship with an older man.

Though it may seem odd, Sophie was not into alcohol or drugs. She had seen too much of that life from her father. But she knew her way around a man, and men seemed to like her for it. Her addiction went deeper than a bottle or a needle. Sophie craved acceptance. No matter that the relationships were purely physical—for a few precious moments, she could pretend that someone cared for her.

Of course, there were rumors of other pregnancies, numerous abortions, many other men, and all sorts of situations that made her more mythical than human. As I later discovered, most of it was urban legend. But the legend grew, and her exploits disgusted some and intrigued others. And as happens with this kind of life, Sophie's skin, not to mention her spirit, thickened. She eventually learned to fight, and to pretend that she didn't care what people thought. Her cryptic, yet somehow menacing, demeanor only added to the mystery of what lay behind those beautiful green eyes and within that wounded heart.

By the time I had my first real conversation with Sophie, her reputation had far outstripped the girl herself. We met in Saturday school. She was there as a result of a fight in which she had shoved another girl's head in a locker. (As a freshman at the time, I had been threatened with this, but gladly found—after some clandestine measuring—that my bucket head would not fit into our school's lockers. Of course, I also spent a great deal of "protection" money making sure that no one tried it. Sophie not only tried it with another girl, she apparently made it work, which led to a suspension, followed by missed school work, which led to Saturday school.)

Saturday school was a familiar place for Sophie. In fact, I believe she held some kind of unofficial record for the most times attended. She would fight or skip class or do something that landed her there time and again. The day was not all bad, though. It was quiet, filled with mostly busy work, but it came with breakfast and lunch and with an instructor who was less excited about being there than us students. This meant that the workload was light, to say the least. Imagine *The Breakfast Club* with a tad more supervision and control.

One ounce of structure we did have was assigned seating. I guess, even though they didn't show much concern for us most of the day, school officials felt that assigned seats might be the difference between learning and not. So, when we arrived, we were assigned a seat, given our worksheets and told to begin.

Oh, maybe I should clear something up—though I'd like you to believe that I was some sort of rebel, I actually attended Saturday school for having missed too many days due to sickness and injury. As a hemophiliac, I spent dozens of days hurt and went before the school board every year to gain permission to pass. No matter that I was an all-A student—rules are rules, and "showing up" was tops on their list. During my freshman year of high school, the Saturday school rule applied to everyone, no matter the excuse, and so on three occasions, I attended. (Didn't want your mind wondering what this neat little Christian boy had done. Now back to the story.)

My assigned seat was next to Sophie. She was three or four years older than me. I knew her reputation (all the boys did), and I sat down with extreme caution, as if she were a tiger. You can only imagine my surprise when I heard her say, "Hi, my name is Sophie. Can you pass me that sheet of paper?" I quickly passed her a standardized sheet in front of me, never making eye contact, convinced that doing so would buy me a ticket to hell. "Thank you," she said.

"Hey . . ." she continued. "Aren't you really smart?"

I didn't know whether or not to respond. *Is she just toying with me? Is this a ploy to lure me into her web?* I muttered something like, "Well, I do okay."

"No," she said. "I hear you're some sort of genius or something."

I had not heard that, but I liked the sound of it. *Wait!* I thought. *This is part of her strategy. Draw you in with flattery and then pounce.* "I do pretty well in school," I finally responded.

"And don't you have a disease?"

Whoa . . . didn't see that coming. Interesting tactic for an evil seduction. "Yeah," I replied. "That's why I am here. I get hurt a lot, miss school and, well . . ."

"You end up at school on Saturday," she finished for me.

I remember looking directly at her for the first time, and noticing her eyes. They really were beautiful—surrounded by too much makeup, but beautiful nonetheless.

"Yeah," I said. "Looks like I am going to be here several times."

"Don't sweat it," she replied. "It's not that bad. You get a good lunch and the work is nothing. Besides, it's quieter on Saturday than during the week. No one to bother you . . ." She paused and then said with a wry smile, "Except for nosey seat mates, huh?" She laughed and then began to write something.

"Why are you here?" I asked, trying to be courteous with the same questions she had asked me, though I knew very well the answer.

"This girl has been giving me a hard time, pushing my buttons and all. I finally got tired of her sh—." She stopped, embarrassed. Every time someone uses profanity in front of me and then realizes what they've done, the scene is always amusing. I've always had this effect on people, even long before ordination.

"Sorry about that," she said. "My mouth gets the best of me sometimes." She smiled and so did I.

Thinking of Sophie shoving the girl's head in a locker, I muttered, "Well, I don't think you have to worry about her bothering you anymore."

"You know," Sophie said with a sarcastic edge, "she's been real nice lately." She smiled again. I did, too. Nervously.

And yet, I remember thinking, *Sophie just smiled and made a joke . . . and not once threatened to shove my head in a locker. And it was a nice smile, too.* This was certainly not the Sophie I had watched and heard about. No, she seemed *normal,* and she seemed relieved to be there, even sitting next to someone like me.

That day, Sophie and Shane became friends. No kidding . . . we genuinely hit it off. I got over her reputation and found a girl who was smarter than she put on, nicer than others believed and easier to know than people cared to discover. And contrary to popular belief, Sophie was not a slacker. Her grades and school work did not reflect her potential or ability. No, they reflected the fact that she worked two part-time jobs in order to pay her way. Working until 11 P.M. every night, plus the weekends, provided little time for study. But in her situation, she had no choice. As my uncle used to say, "People gotta make a living."

By the end of the day, Sophie seemed at ease with me, without the façade she wore most of the time; and, mostly because of her, I enjoyed the day, too.

The bell rang and it was time to leave. "See you next Saturday," Sophie said. She packed her things and left the room.

Next Saturday? I thought. *We'll see each other every day during the week . . . won't we? Oh yeah . . . she's a senior and I'm freshman, and never the twain shall meet. How rude!*

Then it hit me. Even after such a good day, Sophie assumed that good little Christian boys just didn't associate with girls like her when everyone else was watching, no matter how much they hit it off.

Wow.

Who Is to Blame?

When I think about Sophie, I wonder, *Who is to blame?* And the same question always seems to be the first in my mind when I read about the woman caught in adultery. It is easy to blame her. She doesn't have much of a defense; she has been caught in the act and she doesn't deny the charges. No, the only thing that saves her is Jesus, whose few wise, quick-witted words make the woman's accusers feel guilty enough to walk away. Any other woman in any other square with any other teacher but Jesus, and things would have turned out very differently.

But back to the question: Is the woman the only one to blame in this story? I'm not much of an expert on adultery, but I know enough to realize that adultery doesn't happen alone. For every adulterer, there is a willing accomplice. Yet the woman is the only one dragged to the street. Was one of her accusers also a customer? Who knows?

I get the feeling that Jesus knew the woman's predicament. Sure, she's not exactly living a noble life, but what has driven her here? It's almost certain that she had not chosen this path. Was it her only option? Scripture doesn't say, yet history reminds us that women in Jesus' day were grossly undervalued, and those who couldn't find a suitable husband and family often resorted to other means for making a living. For every bad decision, there is a series of bad decisions, made by more than one person, leading up to it. This woman's sin was not her choice alone. No, it took place within a relationship, alongside the choices of her accomplice. But, as happens so many times in situations like this, she is alone, abandoned, when she lands in the dust at Jesus' feet. I imagine that Jesus more than knows the depth of her sin, but He also knows that her abandonment issues, rooted in the bad decisions of others, are part of the problem.

Let me say again for those of you needing to cling to this point: The woman was guilty. She had committed sins against herself and grievances against the faith. The Law prescribed death for such a trespass. But where the letter of the Law stops, Jesus begins. One lesson Jesus teaches throughout His ministry is that sin does not happen in a vacuum; we are interconnected to the core of our lives. Jesus' confrontation with the woman's accusers opens the door for a new kind of spiritual conversation, one rarely heard in the legalistic religion they practiced.

No one in the crowd understands the Law better than Jesus. In fact, He understands not only the Law but also the way the woman's accusers are trying to use it to trap Him. The Law in its most elementary form attempts to confront sin and eradicate its impact. Read within the context of the Jewish faith and culture, there is nothing wrong with the purpose of the Law. Truth is never the problem, right? If you have ever had to confront adultery face to face, you understand how painful and destructive it is. It affects not only the individuals involved; it has a dramatic impact on an entire community. Who wouldn't want to drive adultery from our midst?

But this encounter isn't just about adultery, at least not the kind committed between two individuals. This is about human nature, and I am not talking about sexuality or desire. No, I mean something even more dangerous: the twistedness of human nature that divides us from our brothers and sisters by convincing us that our condemning thoughts, feelings and actions can be justified for personal survival. Let me ask you, *What is the worst kind of adultery?* The act committed by two people caught in a sexual relationship, or the adultery committed against God when we believe that we can pronounce His judgment on our brothers and sisters? In doing so, do we not make ourselves our own god? And, in doing that, do we not replace God with someone else? Isn't that cheating on God? Isn't that the definition of adultery? I believe Jesus would say yes.

As the scene develops, Jesus begins to write in the dirt. What is this all about? Is He biding His time? Is it a rabbinic trick? Or does Jesus' action symbolize what He knows—that the dirty details of the woman's sin can't hold a candle to the filth encrusting the hearts of those around her?

It's worth noting that Jesus answers the accusers' questions, but never disagrees with the part of the Law they so dearly want Him to recognize. In fact, He confirms its seriousness and then takes it one step further: "If any one of you is without sin, let him be the first to throw a stone at her" (John 8:7). His reply stops the self-righteous leaders in their tracks. Scripture describes them dropping their stones one by one, beginning with the oldest, as though the more mature among them understands what Jesus is doing: With one sentence, He affirms the Law and reminds everyone of its intended purpose.

Man, I like this guy!

You see, friend, Jesus understood that the woman was not the only person in need of a new start. She wasn't the only one suffering from a sickness that doctors couldn't heal. The woman was not the only lost and forgotten soul who needed to see the light that the Good News announced. No, Jesus understood that the woman's story was the story of every person surrounding her that day, and the story of each of us today. The grace of Christ doesn't just reach for those lying in the dirt; it reaches for those of us who choose to stand in judgment. Jesus knew the woman, but He knew her accomplice and He knew the accusers, too.

I believe God grows weary of our need to hurt and condemn one another in such quick fashion, especially given the state of our own souls. He knows that we all need to be freed from the bondage of our sinful choices and the bad decisions of others.

Let me give you an example. My wife and I have an amazing marriage . . . now. It has not always been so. For several years while I pastored a new church, our marriage nearly unraveled. One day we awoke to realize that we were held hostage by mistakes and misguided intentions. Although we had not committed the same sin as the woman, Pokey and I both found ourselves lying in the dirt at the feet of Jesus. Ironically, we stood in judgment, too—stones in hand, ready to pummel one another. In fact, as we looked closer at the story of the woman caught in adultery, we discovered a bit of ourselves in every character. It was unnerving. But we also realized some powerful truths about our marriage and about our faith. Taking the time to assess our dusty conditions and wonder if we really were prepared to throw those stones made us see how much more we wanted, how much more we needed in God. It was a difficult time, but confronting it together in the love of Christ changed our marriage forever.

Let me be clear: God does not like sin. God does not like adultery. God does not like the pain we cause each other. But God also doesn't like us to decide what each other's fate will be. No, that decision belongs to God; He alone makes that call.

And if Jesus' encounter with the woman caught in adultery is any indication, that is reason for hope.

"Where have your accusers gone?" Jesus asks her. In doing so, He clears the path of her sin, her rejection, her loneliness, her pain and her past, so that she can see and take hold of a new and better way. The first step to freedom in Christ, whether we're lying in the dirt or hefting a rock in our hand—or both—is to turn away from the past toward the future God intends for us.

Saturdays with Sophie

Sophie and I met for three Saturdays in a row. Each time, I found her more at ease, and I felt that we had become genuine friends. Our interactions at school during the week also increased, first a smile or nod of the head, then conversations at break. Soon we were having lunch under the breezeway in front of the building.

Our conversations deepened; we talked about things other than school, fights and suspensions. I still couldn't quite understand why she liked me; given her reputation and the fact that I was a freshman, any sort of friendship appeared odd at best. But I suspected that maybe Sophie liked talking to someone who didn't want anything from her. I was not her type (whatever that might have been), and I knew the hard knocks life could throw at you. I didn't understand her situation with family and friends (or lack thereof), but I did know a thing or two about being "different" and about dealing with issues that kids don't usually have to confront.

Maybe another value to our friendship was that I didn't try to fix her. I have played the role of fixer in my life, and found that it is not productive. I have discovered that "fixing" someone is more about the ego of the fixer than helping the one who needs to be fixed. Besides, Sophie didn't need fixing—she needed someone to discover who she really was. As she opened up about one situation or another, I kept telling her that God loved her, that she was worth something to Him, and that I would pray for her to feel and experience that truth. She would chuckle and then say, "I know, Shane." This was usually followed by her grabbing me in a bear hug, much like holding on to a stuffed animal. She would then whisper something about how "sweet" I was with an I-hope-you-are-right nervous laugh. Sophie liked that someone cared about her, though she found humor in what she considered my naïve and simple approach to life.

Before long, I found myself defending her to other people. She was nothing like her reputation, even though she admitted that many of the rumors were true. Yet I could tell by the way she spoke about her life that she lived two lives, one fashioned out of her need to survive and the other a deeper, truer expression of who she really was. Sophie dreamed the same dreams as every other girl I knew. She wanted to be liked, to have a boyfriend who treated her well and to expect a future full of possibility. Unfortunately, the bad choices she had made and the bad decisions of others had landed her in the dirt time and time again.

Saturday school ended, but my friendship with Sophie did not. We continued to talk at school, and on occasion (without my family knowing), she drove me home from school. It was during one of these trips that I admitted to Sophie how nervous I had been that first Saturday. I told her about my absurd paranoia, including the whole locker thing. (She got a good laugh out of that.) I also told her about my first impressions of her—about how good Christian boys were not supposed to sit next to girls like her. Suddenly, she wasn't laughing. Her lack of response was not due to anger but sadness.

"You came in the room," I said, "and all of these defenses went up. My holy meter went off the charts, and I acted like a person who confronts a leper, afraid I would catch whatever you had." (I had learned the term "holy meter" in Sunday School when the teacher talked about the gauges God gives us to know right from wrong. I didn't realize until later that the darn thing doesn't work unless it is plugged into the right part of a person's heart.)

"I was wrong," I said, "and I want you to know that I am sorry for thinking those things."

"You don't need to apologize," Sophie responded. "Most of your first impressions were right. Good Christian boys aren't supposed to hang around with girls like me."

"You're wrong!" Sophie's faced changed as I vehemently disagreed. "That's the lie!" I continued. "You are exactly who I needed to be around, not for your sake but for mine."

"I don't understand," she said quietly.

I turned to face her, desperate to explain. "I have been taught about right and wrong my whole life. But right and wrong only from the perspective of what protected me. You've told me about things that happened to you and things you've done, and they all have one thing in common . . . no one stopped to care enough about you. All these good Christian folks . . . and no one could look past your circumstances to see the real pain. Sophie, faith means nothing if we don't have grace."

"You don't talk like a freshman," she said with a chuckle, looking away, out the car window.

"Sophie," I said. "Look at me."

She turned her head, and I noticed the tears in her eyes.

"I didn't mean to say anything wrong..." I began to apologize.

A gentle smile formed as the tears ran down her face. "You didn't say anything wrong, Shane," she replied. "I was just sitting here thinking that this is the first time I've ever sat in a car with a boy and just talked."

Suddenly I was struck, too, by the oddity of the situation. Here I was, a normal teenage boy, sitting in a car with someone who was considered the easiest girl in school, and I was talking about her self-esteem and about how God loves her. I couldn't help but think, *So this is why people think I'm a strange kid.*

Sophie took my hand and pulled me over to her. She kissed me on the cheek and whispered in my ear, "Shane, you're a sweet guy and for some reason you can see good things in people. Don't ever let anyone take that away from you."

She pushed back but kept her face close to mine, and put her hand gently on my cheek. With tears now streaming, she looked me in the eyes and said, "Thank you."

Sophie did not graduate—too many incompletes and suspensions. However, she took the GED, passed and got a job working at a local hospital. Because I no longer saw her at school, we didn't talk much anymore. I saw her occasionally at football games or around town, but a year or two after her senior year, Sophie moved away, finally escaping the difficulties of her home.

As I prepared to write this book, I knew I wanted to tell Sophie's story. After some investigative work, I located Sophie, living in Texas. Following her move there, she had enrolled in nursing school at a local community college and discovered a real passion for the profession, eventually receiving both her bachelor's and master's degrees. Sophie married a fellow nurse who worked at the same hospital, and they are the parents of a beautiful little girl, who is fittingly named Grace.

Sophie gave me permission to share her story, but only if I altered the circumstances enough to protect her and her family. A lot had changed for her over the years, and she preferred to keep the past, in her words, "where it belongs."

"I don't visit there much," Sophie told me. "Either literally or emotionally."

I could understand her reluctance to retell a painful story. From our conversation, I could tell that Sophie approached life much differently now. She spoke with words of faith and hope, and it was clear to me that she liked where, and more importantly, *who* she was.

"I will tell it in a way that will keep the details private," I promised. "I just believe that sharing your story might help someone in a similar situation."

"I trust you to do it right," she said. "It's not that I'm ashamed any longer of my past; it's just not *me* anymore, and sometimes dead things should be left alone."

We talked a bit more, mostly about the years since high school, and we agreed that one day our families needed to meet—though we both knew the busyness of life would make that difficult. The conversation was friendly and familiar.

Just before our goodbyes, Sophie paused and said, "Shane, years ago a friend told me that I needed to discover something I liked and go with it." I remembered giving that advice, but only vaguely. "Well," she continued, "I have discovered something I like very much . . . me. And it has made all the difference."

The Benefit of the Doubt

There are worse things than dying; sometimes, living is much harder. The woman in the dirt at Jesus' feet understood this. So did Sophie. They both experienced spiritual attacks brought on by the Adversary whose intention was to break their hearts. Though the circumstances may be different, many of us experienced attacks meant for the same purpose. The assault may come from an illness, from a bad relationship, from past mistakes, but regardless what form they take, the goal is to so drain our lives of hope that we find ourselves lying in the dirt, wishing the end would come. Some of us, covered in the grime of shame and tasting the grit of regret, even figure it would be easier to die than to live like this.

But Satan doesn't want to kill you—he wants to own you at the lowest bargain price he can negotiate. His trouble is, he can't close the deal alone; he needs your signature on the contract. The woman caught in adultery came close to making the sale. She had convinced herself there was no hope, that she had gone too far for anyone to care. What followed? Self-doubt, self-loathing, self-destruction . . . and hopelessness. Why change? Why bother? The woman, in her feelings, expectations and actions, had become her own worst enemy.

But don't just blame her; she had help. And I'm not just talking about her accomplice in adultery. The entire crowd played a part. How ready they were to stone her! How many of them could have made a difference in the woman's life but turned away instead? Maybe they so feared revealing their own failings that they needed to punish her—partly for her transgressions, sure, but mostly for their own.

Too easily, Satan convinces us to believe the lies we tell ourselves and each other. We don't need the whole story, just enough of the lie to plant a seed of doubt. One seed planted here and another one there, until they have grown into a full-blown patch of weeds, choking every corner of our lives. The weeds take root and become a fixture in our relationships, our thought patterns and our spiritual walk. Finally, after a while, it is difficult to remember what led us here, much less how in the world we escape from such a place.

The way out of these lonely, desperate places is not as difficult as it seems. The Adversary needs us to believe that turning the tide is too risky, that it takes too much effort and is too costly. The truth? It only takes one moment to turn things around. The woman caught in adultery found her moment in the dirt. As one stone after another dropped to the ground, Jesus posed this question: "Woman, where are [your accusers]? Has no one condemned you?" (John 8:10).

When she looked up, she saw that the crowd had gone. "No one condemns me," she uttered (see John 8:11).

"Then neither do I condemn you," Jesus declared (John 8:11).

In that moment, the woman's future changed. She had become accustomed to rejection. She had understood the sneers and stares. She had expected the gossip and hateful whispers. But she had not been prepared for Jesus. He had given her the benefit of the doubt, and it was likely the first time anyone had ever offered her such a gift.

And what an amazing gift it was! To live your entire life with everyone expecting the worst only to find, at the darkest hour, Someone who believes in you. You can't buy it, earn it, trade your body for it. No, it is what it is: an offering of grace that changes the way you view life and its possibilities. It's true that this gift doesn't change the circumstances or details immediately, but it gives you a new starting point, and you can't help but believe that there must be a better way than the one you have traveled.

The world sometimes succeeds in convincing us that certain things are inevitable and that certain patterns created in our lives cannot be changed. *Once trouble, always trouble.* But do you really think God believes it? I don't—too much evidence indicates otherwise. The gospel narrative points again and again in stories like this to God's hope for us, long before we have hope for Him. Jesus' love for you and me, shown in every one of His teachings and interactions, points to the high value God places on each of our lives and the potential He sees in each of us. If we are valuable enough for Jesus to become like us, will He not offer each of us the chance to turn from the past, brush off the dirt and become more like Him?

John 3:16-17 still tells the story of God's intentions for every person lying prone in the dirt of their lives. Let me paraphrase: *God loved us so much that Jesus came to be like us, so that everyone who believes in Him will find real life, now and forever. Oh . . . and if this is the case, then certainly God didn't send Jesus to condemn but to restore us.* This is the heart of the gospel, the hope for the world.

We condemn—ourselves, each other, even God—because it is easier than believing what God has given to us in Christ. Christ's plan is not to condemn. God knows the ease of condemnation—pass judgment, wipe your hands, a day's work done. Instead, Jesus' words to the woman set out the primary principles to guide us in our relationship with God and with others. *I choose not to pass judgment because I am offering a second chance, so that not only will you see the potential of a life restored, but others will, too.* In those few words, Christ offers forgiveness, a challenge and a new beginning.

And critics on both sides are left speechless. Those who rush to judgment find in Jesus a new standard of grace and forgiveness. Those who claim that His "love for sinners" is measured by cheap faith with no accountability find that God expects us to do better. Jesus' forgiveness and restoration of the woman send a signal to everyone: *Sin is serious business in which each person here is employed, and now I'm making it* My *business.* The scene of the woman landing in the dirt at Jesus' feet is personal and uncomfortable because we can't help but see ourselves in one character or another . . . and, like it or not, we're in this together.

If One of Us Can't Play . . .

My neighbor's son is a remarkable young man. Walker is 16 years old and, like many his age, enjoys having a good time. He is popular, good at sports and, as a tall, good-looking kid, has no problem impressing the girls (he would hate that I just wrote that). But there is much more to Walker than meets the eye. He is incredibly polite, hardworking and respectful. He enjoys spending time with his family and always finds time to interact with his younger sister and her friends. Walker is a good kid with all of the qualities that the father of daughters watches for in a boy.

Walker is also active in his local church and has a spiritual aptitude greater than many his age. He has a heart tender toward God and a genuine love for God's people. This maturity of faith led Walker to volunteer with his dad for a mission trip to Costa Rica. The trip was planned to provide recreational ministry to under-resourced children. Their mission station was a local church in the town of San Isidro, a village mostly made up of poor, forgotten families. But the church there has a strong presence in the community, and by all accounts, the people are unbelievably kind, open and giving, even in the midst of their poverty.

Walker's job was to play sports with kids, a task right up his alley. Each day, he gathered the kids and played soccer, basketball and kickball. No matter the language barrier, the laughter and excitement of the children transcended words. During those days he spent with the children, Walker ministered to each child through play and witnessed the power of Christ, even in the dirt of an abandoned soccer field. Walker learned that kids make the most of every moment. Not like adults. Their worlds revolve around the simple things, like fairness, fun and laughter. No, it is not until much later, when they have seen too many adults act otherwise, that they begin to exhibit the broken edges of human nature. Walker found out that children can sometimes teach adults much more than we ever teach them.

One day while playing soccer with the kids in the village, Walker seriously injured his ankle. He limped over to the sidelines.

An elderly lady tended to him with some ointment and a make-shift bandage. The medical treatment was primitive at best. As the woman cared for his wound, Walker noticed that the children had stopped playing. They walked over and sat in a semicircle around him and the woman. They watched quietly as the woman finished the bandage.

"What are you guys doing?" Walker asked the kids. "You should be playing!"

Without relating Walker's words to the children, the translator looked at Walker and said, "It won't matter . . . if you can't play, they won't play either."

In our culture, before the injured are even removed from the field, someone else is in the wings ready to take their place. Stop the game? You must be kidding! The children of San Isidro look more like Christ. They know that *we're in this together.*

In the Dirt with the Woman
Caught in Adultery

In his wonderful book *The Ragamuffin Gospel*, Brennan Manning writes:

> After long hours of prayer and meditation on the Scriptures and reflection on the nagging question "Who Am I?" a gracious God has given me the light to see myself as I really am. I now have a primary identity and a coherent sense of myself. It affects my intimacy with God, my relationships with others, and my gentleness with myself.[1]

If you, like Brennan and like the woman caught in adultery, feel as if you are living in the dirt, I have a question for you: Would you like another chance, maybe a new start? Then stop throwing stones at yourself, and stop repeating the same choices that land you at Jesus' feet time and again. You were meant for more than this. Christ knows it; you should, too. Don't sell your soul at a bargain price. Lift your head and look around. Where are your accusers? God believes in second chances. Do you?

If, on the other hand, you are standing in the crowd—as an accuser or just a curious bystander—let me tell you this: Many of our brothers and sisters feel God's absence because we help them to believe it by our rejection, sneers, gossip or indifference. People believe the lies when no one bothers to tell them the truth. Will you really be the first to throw a stone?

Whether we are lying in the dirt or practicing our aim, Jesus asks, *Wouldn't you rather stop the game? Here is one of your own in trouble—if she can't play, shouldn't we all sit this one out?*

This encounter places each of us in the picture. We see the best and worst of ourselves, and it is time to decide who we will be in this world. The crowd has gathered around, the accusers are waiting. The dirt is hot and dusty. But this is not a game, and the stones will do damage. My sister, lying in the dirt—and my brother, the stone in your hand—what will it be?

Note

1. Brennan Manning, *The Ragamuffin Gospel* (Sisters, OR: Multnomah Publishers, Inc., 2005).

5

The Fifth Encounter:
Mary, Martha and Lazarus

JOHN 11:1-44

Some . . . think that God is a Wizard-of-Oz or Sistine Chapel kind of being
sitting at a location very remote from us. . . .
Of such a "god" we can only say, "Good riddance!"

DALLAS WILLARD, *THE DIVINE CONSPIRACY*

I was in the first year of starting a new church when I announced to the congregation on Sunday that I needed some office volunteers. Starting a new congregation often means serving not only as pastor but also as secretary, education director, children and youth minister, and janitor. Our little congregation, which had started with 30 people, had grown quickly, and I was in need of support.

On Monday morning, an attractive woman in her late 40s walked into the office. She was tall and thin and appeared unsteady when she walked. Yet she also had a certain grace that made her gait seem more methodical than laborious. She also had beautiful red hair and a delightful smile, as well as a sternness in her eyes that reminded me of my mother, especially when I was in trouble.

"Hi, my name is Carol," she said. "I've come to volunteer."

"Well, thank you. I could certainly use the help," I responded. "What would you like to help with?"

"I can do most anything," Carol said. "I like to organize and type . . . you know, the basic office stuff."

I gave Carol a stack of envelopes that needed to be addressed and stamped. "Do you mind getting these ready to mail?" I asked.

"Not at all," Carol replied. She sat down at our makeshift conference table and got to work.

An hour later, Carol had finished and returned to ask for more to do. I had thought that the mailing project would keep her busy the entire morning.

"Is that the best you can do?" she said, holding back a smile.

"Oh, I think I can challenge you," I said smugly. I liked bantering with her, especially since most days I was alone in our temporary little office.

I handed her a stack of visitor cards and asked her to alphabetize a list of names and file the cards according to attendance date.

One hour later, Carol returned, having completed the list. She had also subdivided the list according to geographic location, dates visited, size of family and type of information requested from the church. She plopped the information on my desk and returned to her seat at the conference table. I took a minute to look at the information, and glanced up to see Carol reading a book in the next room. On my third glance, she said, without looking at me, "When you think of something for me to do, please let me know. I'll be right here."

And right there she stayed until 5 P.M. that afternoon. When she gathered her stuff to leave, she poked her head into my office and said, "I can only come on Mondays and Wednesdays. I will be here at 8:30 A.M. sharp and will stay the entire day. Let me know what you need me to do." And with that, Carol left.

All day Tuesday, I worried over what to give Carol to do on Wednesday. I thought of every conceivable task, menial and major, that might keep her busy. When she arrived the next morning, she immediately began work on my neatly crafted to-do list. I sat back, sure that I had given her more than enough to last the day.

She finished before noon.

"Would you like some lunch?" she asked, standing at the door of my office.

"Yes," I said, a little startled.

"I will get you a turkey sandwich on wheat," she replied. "That will be healthy for you. And oh, by the way . . . I am finished with your list." She turned and walked toward the door. I guess she didn't realize that I could see her face in the mirror in the hall; she had a smirk the size of Texas. (Come to think of it . . . maybe she *did* realize I could see.)

I raced to the conference area where she had been working and found every task not only completed, but completed *perfectly*.

This is no ordinary volunteer, I thought. *There is more to Carol than meets the eye.*

She returned 30 minutes later with two turkey sandwiches, a bag of baked potato chips and two diet Sprites. I don't like potato chips or diet Sprites, and I'm not too crazy about turkey sandwiches, either. But I ate all of it. Carol scared me.

I began to wonder, *What have I gotten myself into here?* Was Carol one of those eccentric people who do good work but become controlling and difficult to be around? Or did she have bizarre and strange habits, such as needing the hand towels hung perfectly parallel or the can labels turned the same way or the books arranged by subject instead of alphabetized by author last name? *Oh, Lord,* I thought, *I have a mad woman on my hands!*

Wait a minute . . . the voice in the back of my mind finally kicked in with a little reason. *You have got to stop drinking so much caffeine and watching late-night television.* The voice was right. I was wound tighter than a preacher's girdle at an all-you-can-eat pancake breakfast (which is pretty tight, in case you're wondering). It had been a tough few weeks. Starting a church was difficult business, and it had taken a toll on me and my family. Truth was, I needed help, and here in front of me was the answer. And instead of falling on my knees in thanks, I sat there making my only volunteer out to be a cross between Woody Allen and the axe-wielding woman in that terrifying Stephen King novel that they made into that even more terrifying movie starring Kathy Bates.

At that moment, in the midst of my somewhat disturbing internal monologue, Carol asked, "Are you okay?"

"No, not really," I admitted. "It has been a tough summer. I was sick a few months ago and my wife is pregnant with our first child and I am starting this new church and I haven't had any training and . . ."

"Whoa! Slow down," Carol said. "You are starting to breathe in run-on sentences."

I laughed. She did, too. I caught myself thinking, *Well, if nothing else, you have a nice laugh for an axe murderer.*

"I understand something about stress," Carol added. "I have chronic pancreatitis; actually, my pancreas is shutting down."

"I'm sorry," I said.

"Don't be sorry. You didn't do it." We laughed again. "And that may be part of your problem," Carol continued. "You seem to feel like everything is either your fault or your responsibility right now." She was right. I did feel that way.

"I like your preaching," she said, changing the subject. "You are the real deal. I also like the way you talk about your illness and struggles. Makes those of us who are going through difficult times feel like we have someone who knows us and understands our situation."

"I certainly try to understand," I said. "I told the District Superintendent that I would only start the church if I could be honest and open with the congregation from the beginning."

"You'd think that would be a given with any church," Carol replied.

"Well, things are a little complicated for me . . . or shall I say, I make them complicated for the 'powers that be'."

"I thought there was only one *Power* that needed worrying over in your line of work?" Carol said.

I raised my eyebrows and shrugged. "Doesn't matter what line of work you're in—people complicate life."

We continued our conversation for several minutes and then cleaned up from lunch. "What do you need me to do now?" Carol asked.

"I am not sure I have anything else," I replied. "Are you sure you want to volunteer here?" I was still puzzled why someone of her ability would settle for being an office volunteer in a small church without a building.

"Look . . . I have spent a lot of time over the past few years asking for something to do," Carol responded. "I told God that if He'd give me something to get up for in the morning, He could count on me to work." She paused and then added, "I believe in you, Shane, and in what God is doing through you."

She never looked up, continuing to clean up the remains of lunch. "I will be here on Fridays now, too," she announced. "Lord knows you need the help."

I couldn't have agreed more.

Friends in Bethany

When we read the Gospels, it is easy for us to think of Jesus walking and teaching around the Palestinian countryside as His band of disciples merrily follows behind. I call Him "Touring Jesus." In this version, the Twelve and Jesus travel from one venue to another, stopping long enough on the mountainside, along the shore or under a tree to dispense the word of wisdom for the day or to perform a miracle. But in reality, the Gospels present a very different picture of Jesus' ministry.

First of all, the travel conditions were wearying and cumbersome, and Jesus' ministry territory stretched from one end of Jewish Palestine to another, occasionally even crossing into Gentile territories. As a traveling preacher, Jesus would have experienced a lot of discomfort. Sure, He was God, but He was also fully human. I'm sure He smelled, felt and acted like any weary traveler. Not exactly the clean and shiny image we have of the Messiah.

Second, like any other traveler of His era, Jesus relied on the kindness of friends and supporters for the basic necessities. Scripture tells us that Jesus did not have a place to call His own (see Matt. 8:20; Luke 9:58), but instead counted on the hospitality of others to provide food, rest and relaxation (see Mark 14:22-25; Luke 10:38). Given the geography Jesus' ministry covered, it was convenient for Him to have certain places He stayed whenever He was in a particular area. The home of Mary, Martha and Lazarus in Bethany was one such place.

Third, because of His reliance on these stops and given the nomadic nature of Jesus' ministry back and forth across Palestine, He would have stopped frequently in these places. And, given such frequent visits, the relationships He developed with these particular followers would have been significant.

Scripture tells us that Jesus felt at home with Mary, Martha and Lazarus (see Luke 10:38-42; John 12:1-8). We can't be sure how and why they came to play such an important role in His ministry, but their support of and dedication to Jesus is unquestionable. Some accounts place Mary (possibly as a troubled young woman or even a person of ill repute) at the center of Jesus' connection to the family. Yet it's clear from the Gospels that Jesus loved not only Mary but also her sister and brother, and theirs was an enduring friendship.

But this was more than a personal relationship. The family supported Jesus' ministry and vocation, and they hosted, on at least one occasion, others who came to hear Jesus teach (see Luke 10:38-42). Their home was more than a stopover for

His travels; it was a teaching center as well.

Jesus treated this family from Bethany as friends and considered them an important part of His ministry and life. It is clear that as much as they needed Jesus, Jesus also needed them, and He appreciated their care for Him and His disciples.

Jesus built enduring relationships that went beyond the roles of teacher and student. We can't picture Jesus only as the rabbi marching through Galilee spouting lessons for living. No, He built real relationships. Jesus had friends.

Think about that for a moment. It is an important concept that many modern believers miss.

If Jesus had friends, then He loved some folks more deeply than others (admit it . . . that idea makes you nervous!). I'm not referring to the grand, cosmic Love that God has for each one of us, Love that by it's very nature cannot be more or less or play favorites; I'm talking about the love that any human has for another, especially if they have shared profound moments of success and struggle. It stands to reason that if Jesus was fully human, as the Scriptures insist, and if He had people in His life who supported and cared for Him during His ministry, then He would have a deeper, personal connection to those folks.

I tried out this theory on several minister friends of mine recently, and they reacted like jealous girlfriends. I was completely unprepared for how they resisted the notion that Jesus could have loved some friends more than others. When I asked them why the idea bothered them so much, they responded with theological arguments, including the impeccably logical (and my personal favorite), "Well, He's Jesus."

When I went so far as to point out that in *our* ministries we are all guilty of having parishioners to whom we feel closer than others, one friend, who may be the smartest of all of us, froze spiritually (you could see it on his face) and was only able to utter, "But we are human."

"Well, wasn't Jesus supposed to be human like us?" I questioned.

"Yes, but . . ." he replied.

"But what?" I countered. "If Jesus was human, then wouldn't He have loved some people more than others? What are you so worried about?" I asked.

My friend stood silent for a moment and then answered, "I'm just not sure that I like Jesus being *that* human."

The conversation got me thinking: If Jesus was human enough to need resources and a place to sleep during His earthly ministry, that means Jesus needed people to provide assistance. And if Jesus needed people, then the ones who responded to His needs would naturally see a more intimate side of Him. And if they saw a more intimate side of a fully human Jesus, then would they not also experience the depth of His response for their care? And, at such depths of personal relationship, would not Jesus call them friends? I mean *real* friends. Not just a "friend of God" friend, but an "I've got your back" friend?

As you know, there is a difference, and that difference affects us in profound ways. "I've got your back" friendships shape who we are and form the heart of what matters in our lives. I don't believe it was any different for Jesus. Jesus needed people. He needed friends. I believe that Mary, Martha and Lazarus were these kinds of friends to Jesus, and I believe He needed them and loved them very much.

The first lesson of this encounter is that Jesus needed people. Jesus had friends.

Jesus teaches us that relationships are more than momentary connections; they mirror the very essence of who God created us to be. He not only talked about these connections, but He also lived them in His friendships with people like Mary, Martha and Lazarus. (And if such friendships are to mean anything in this world, they must also weather a hairline fracture or two in order to become invulnerable to change, disruption and even death. More about that in a minute.)

I have asked you this question before, but let me ask it again: *Why was it necessary for Jesus to walk among us in order to redeem us?* Could it be that Jesus had to make friends and see imperfections and feel loss, just like us, in order to accomplish His mission? Jesus always goes to the heart of what we dread in this world. We dread being alone, so we make friends. We dread being hurt, so we don't make friends. We dread feeling betrayed, so we don't let our real selves show. We dread loss, so we choose not to love. If Jesus' friendships teach us nothing else, they remind us that He understands the intrinsic needs, wounds and fears of our lives.

Four Reactions

Why all the talk about Jesus and friends and mushy stuff? What about the dead guy?

Right, Lazarus! We're getting to him.

If you read the Scripture passage prior to reading this chapter (if not, now is a good time!), you know that we have a dead guy (probably pretty content where he is), two very upset sisters and a bunch of confused bystanders, not the least of whom are the disciples. Jesus has tarried just long enough that Lazarus has not only died but has been dead for some while, leaving most Jews to believe that his soul had departed the body. The religious leaders are mocking Jesus for not being everywhere at the same time (a precursor to the modern pastor-layperson relationship), and Thomas, God love him, is making proclamations about following Jesus to his death. (Thomas is an optimist.)

Where are you going with this? Let's get to the miracle already! Patience, my friend. Zeroing in on the wrong thing is where most of us get into trouble.

When God seems to have vanished, when we feel completely alone, we have a tendency to believe one of two things. First, we believe that God and God's people *can't* love us. Or second, we believe that God and God's people *don't* love us. And when that happens, we retreat into some kind of junior-high self-preservation instinct that tells us we either need to run or fight because the situation has no solution.

Yet the earthly life of Christ, wrapped within the mysteries of what God was doing cosmically, points to some practical principles that God wants us to remember when the world is caving in on us. Jesus' ministry counters what the world would have us believe: *You must do it alone; you have to have a certain kind of smarts or be a certain kind of religious.*

For some reason, we tend to believe those voices in the back of our minds that say we have to be a certain way in order to have value or purpose. Of course, nothing could be farther from what Jesus lives and teaches. Watch who He makes friends with and see how those friendships show what He values (the Beatitudes, for example, tell us a lot about the folks Jesus considered friends). The friends Jesus makes tell us more about Him and us and the whole world than any Scripture, worship service or liturgy ever could. And when the going gets tough, Jesus' friendships remind us of a few indispensable notions that the Adversary would rather us forget—namely that humanity is wired for us to care for each other and do life together, because the Great Wirer, God, made us in His image. Relationships are why we are formed and how we experience, enjoy and survive the ups and downs of this place.

If such is the case, it's no surprise that relationships are the heart and soul of this encounter, which occurs because of great loss, the loss of a loved one. This loss leads several of Jesus' friends, previously unshakeable in their faith, to acutely feel God's absence. Truth be told, I don't believe this encounter and the subsequent miracle are just about Christ raising someone from the dead; in many ways, the miracle serves as the back story to the passage's real meaning. (Lazarus being raised from the dead may not even be in the top three reasons to take note of what happens here. Why? Because this is not primarily a lesson about being raised from the dead like Lazarus; it is more about *living* like Lazarus after he was raised.)

I believe the key verse in this passage is "Jesus wept" (John 11:35). But *why* did He weep? Did death affect Him that much? It would be naïve to think that Lazarus was the first person in Jesus' life who had died. Did He question whether or not He could raise Lazarus? Scripture tells us that He had already performed such a miracle for a Temple leader's daughter (see Mark 5:35-43) and a young man from Nain (see Luke 7:11-17). Did he fear the repercussions of a miracle such as this?

The Gospel of John hints that the resurrection of Lazarus catalyzed the plot to kill Jesus, but the other Gospels say that it was more a perceived threat to the authority of the Pharisees from Jesus' rising popularity that sealed His fate. Given the other passages, raising someone from the dead alone didn't condemn Jesus. Yet if these were not the reasons, why did Jesus stand and weep at the grave of His friend? Further, the passage doesn't say He "teared up" or "felt misty eyed"; it says He *wept*. To understand what could bring such raw emotion from Jesus, we must go deeper, look inside the situation and seek to understand the real story happening in and around this tomb.

The key to understanding this encounter rests in watching Jesus confront the folks involved—the disciples (Thomas in particular), Mary and Martha, and, lest we forget, Lazarus—paying attention to their various reactions, and then watching Jesus respond. We will see that their reactions have less to do with Lazarus's death and everything to do with their own fears, beliefs and anxieties. I think you'll also see that our reactions in moments such as these say less about our grief than they do about our expectations of God in the midst of it.

The Disciples

Let's look at the disciples first. When the disciples heard that Lazarus was ill, they were already feeling overwhelmed by fear and anxiety. Jesus had angered the Establishment and He was now a marked man. The disciples didn't want to go back to Bethany, which was near Jerusalem and the religious leaders who had it in for Jesus, and they had (conveniently?) allowed Him to tarry for a couple of days before they set off. After all, the last time they were in Bethany, things didn't turn out well; the Jewish leaders had plotted to kill them. Jesus' returning to Bethany was, in the disciples' minds, not a wise move. If Jesus wanted to wait, fine with them; a "sleeping" friend didn't seem like a good excuse to risk life and limb.

It's not a stretch to say that the disciples downplayed Lazarus's need of Jesus. The word for "sleep" in Jesus' day had a dual meaning, and though the disciples were more than happy to interpret it as "slumber," given the context, they must have known there was more to it. Still, it was easier to convince themselves that Lazarus was napping than to face the danger of going back. Of course, some were obviously afraid for Jesus, but others of them were afraid for themselves.

While it's interesting that the disciples reacted to news of Lazarus's condition this way, it is not surprising. This is the tendency for many of us when things get uncomfortable or discouraging. The disciples retreated to a convenient excuse. When Jesus pushed the need to go further, their anxiety heightened. It is a story played out in our lives every day. Case in point: I have a friend who hates conflict. In fact, he will do whatever is necessary to avoid confrontation. Sometimes he allows himself to believe the most absurd excuses or explanation as a way of validating his unwillingness to resolve a dispute. In the end, the conflict only worsens and his anxiety increases. He eventually finds himself confronting the situation anyway, having only postponed the inevitable and made himself sick with worry in the meantime.

Jesus won't let the disciples get away with similar delay tactics. He wants to teach them a lesson about *time* and *courage*. He talks with them about "twelve hours in a day" (see John 11:9) because He wants the disciples to see the importance not just of time, but of *their* time, and He illustrates the proper, timely way to respond when God calls. It is easy to follow our natural instincts and retreat, allowing our fears and uncertainties to get the best of us—to spend time doing nothing but worrying. Yet what does God intend for how we use our time?

First, Jesus explains that God's time is perfectly set. Our work for God is never useless or in vain (see 1 Cor. 15:58). Returning to Bethany is not only the right thing to do, but it is also God's intention for them. Second, if God's timing is perfect, then they are equipped to respond with courage, trusting that God goes before them. Finally, as Jesus raises the temperature of the conversation, He implies that not only are they equipped to respond, they are *expected* to respond. Essentially, there is no more time to waste; one way or another, Jesus is headed toward Bethany, with or without the disciples.

Friends, we can't miss this point. God's plan often leads us into difficult situations. Regardless of the difficulty, God has made a way for us and we are expected to move forward. When we fail to respond to God's plan in our lives, we create a tension, not between God and us, but within ourselves. Most of us know when we have not done what is needed. We can excuse it or explain it away, but ultimately we must confront the truth of what it is: our predisposition to protect our selfish interests at the expense of God's work in our lives.

The reaction of the disciples shows us that when the forecast is bleak and danger is just over the horizon, some choose survival and run the other way.

Thomas

In announcing that He would leave for Bethany, Jesus did what any friend would do. Yes, He had waited, but the passage never suggests that Jesus did not plan to go at all. Yet His delay gave rise to the question, in the minds of the disciples, of whether He would go or not. Listening to their debate, it might sound as if all of them felt the same way about Jesus returning to Bethany. That is, until Thomas spoke up.

Scripture portrays Thomas as passionate, emotional and skeptical. Most of us are familiar with Thomas's encounter following the Resurrection, when he asked to touch the scars of Jesus. He needed facts. His doubts were not about a lack of faith; on the contrary, Thomas's faith was great. No, his doubts were about getting enough information to ensure that he chose the right steps, no matter where they might lead. Regardless of our perception of him, Thomas was a responder; he just *qualified* his responses before making decisions. Thus, we shouldn't discount or be surprised by Thomas's willingness and courage in following Jesus to Bethany. Not only was he prepared to go with Jesus, Thomas was prepared for whatever might come, including giving his own life. Thomas's courage is admirable; at least he took a stand for Jesus' decision. The disciples largely lacked courage; Thomas did not. No, Thomas lacked hope.

I have known many in my ministry who possess a strong sense of courage, but who have not experienced real hope. God wants both for us. A church member recently reminded me of the difference. During a Bible study meeting, I shared my experiences with heart surgery, and after the class that evening, a church member told me that she, too, had faced some difficult times in her life. As she weathered the storms and made her way through, she not only found courage to endure the event, she also realized that God intended for her to prevail in wonderful and unexpected ways.

She described in great detail how her life had fallen apart, affecting most of her relationships. Because of this stress, her physical health also failed, until finally she had lost almost everything. One night, however, while praying that God would either give her strength to survive or let her die (that's how bad the situation was), God audibly spoke to her. The words were from Jeremiah 29:11: "'I know the plans I have for you,' declares the Lord, 'plans to prosper you and not to harm you, plans to give you hope and a future.'"

"It was in that moment," she said, "that I claimed the promise for my life that I didn't serve a God of *getting by* but a God of *going on to something better*." The language may seem flowery, but this particular church member did not use words lightly. She believed and lived as a person of hope.

I asked her if the situation had resolved itself as she wanted, and to my surprise, she said no. I stood back a minute, wondering where this was going, having assumed this would be a perfect story wrapped up in a bow and ready to be trotted out whenever I next needed an illustration about triumphing through struggle.

"It turned out better than I could have expected," she said. "What I had been praying was that God would give me the strength to endure. Instead, He gave me the hope to prevail." A beautiful expression crossed her face as she spoke those words. She was still amazed by what God had done. For a moment, I thought about how so often we forget to be amazed by the living God working in us.

"I don't want the details in one of your books," she said with a smile. "Just tell people that God has bigger plans for us than survival."

This conversation reminded me that God does not need us to join the "faith forces" and head into battle, although there are times when simple, grit-your-teeth courage is needed. No, God has better in store for us, and the better is abundance . . . now! We should not forget that even in the midst of our struggles, "in all things God works for the good of those who love him" (Rom. 8:28).

Thomas reacted with great courage, and we should applaud that, but God has more in store for us.

Martha

When Jesus arrived in Bethany, He found a house full of mourners. This was not uncommon. In Jesus' day, when people died, family and friends were moved to action. Mourning was not sedentary; it involved a response both emotional and physical. Jesus would have encountered these mourners already gathered for a long period of remembrance and ritual.

He would have also arrived to questions about why He was so late. Bethany was only a few miles away from where Jesus and the disciples had been, yet they did not arrive until the fourth day after Lazarus's death. I won't spend much time on the reaction of the crowd, because there is little evidence of what was actually said. But we all know human nature. As Jesus arrived, there would have been whispers about why such a close friend had not responded sooner. It's nothing new, and nothing has changed. There have always been and will always be those who, when the worst happens, presume to know what someone else's intentions really were and should have been. They are the Monday-morning quarterbacks of the Church who feel emboldened, almost compelled, to share an opinion or pronounce a verdict on a case about which they have no real knowledge. These folks are like flies at a picnic—maybe not enough to derail God's work, but annoying enough to disgust it.

Why is this important? Because no situation in our lives happens in a vacuum. Good or bad, our circumstances are affected by others—and vice versa. That is one of the results of being created to need one another and of being wired together in community. Community can spark the best of what God has created in us, but it can also unveil the worst.

This is where we find Martha, surrounded by friends and family, yet in the center of much anxiety and sorrow. Any of us who have faced the death of a loved one or friend knows the stress of these situations and the incredible sense of spiritual disruption that comes with it.

When Martha hears of Jesus' arrival, her reaction fits with her personality and provides a lesson for many of us like her. Martha is a person of action. Her brother is dead and she feels the need to solve the problem of her pain. She couldn't save him, but that doesn't alleviate her need to save *something*. Does this sound familiar? She needs to fix something, do something or make something, all in an effort to distract from the problem and numb the pain. Scripture does not detail it, but I can imagine the frenzy Martha is in as she goes through the obligatory mourning period.

Jesus' arriving is a relief to Martha, but it's also one more "responsibility" for her. Remember, she is a caretaker. Although Jesus, her friend, is here and could possibly provide answers to her many questions, Martha does not ask why this all has happened and, more importantly, why Jesus did not come sooner. Instead, Martha approaches Jesus as the good mourner/follower/hostess. What she really wants to ask is "Why?" but Martha reacts to Jesus as many of us act with God. She really wants to ask, "Why weren't you . . . ?" "What happened?" "I thought you were a friend." But like Martha, rather than honestly asking the questions we need or want to know the answers to, we play nice: "I know if you had been here . . ."

Even after Jesus answers her with some of the most important words in all of the Gospel texts—"I am the resurrection and
the life" (John 11:25)—Martha continues the pattern by giving an
academic answer about resurrection. Again Martha is not honest
about her feelings. Why? The answer lies in what I call "spiritual
politeness disorder" (I just made that up, actually). I believe that,
in most situations, we know very well what we are feeling; we just
aren't willing to be honest with ourselves and with God. But how
can we have real conversations about real issues in our lives and
about our deepest emotions if we are unwilling to honestly approach God with our questions and disappointments?

Martha's reaction is like some of the answers I have given
when I have ministered to families in difficult situations who
ask why God has allowed a particular event to happen. For in-
stance, several years ago, a family in my congregation lost a
young child to SIDS. It was one of the most difficult situations
I have ever encountered. As I sat with the family, the father asked
why this had happened. Feeling the need to respond in some
way, and asking myself the same question, I gave a very academic
answer, which boiled down to a defense of God and His sover-
eignty. The father looked at me politely but with little emotion.
Thankfully, at that moment someone walked up and I was able
to finish by asking the father if I could "get you anything."

Later, as we were leaving the home of the family, our
church's minister of visitation, who was a retired layperson,
said, "Can I ask you something?"

"Sure," I responded.

"Why didn't you just say you didn't know when the father
asked why this happened?"

I paused, wanting to be honest with him. "I don't know,"
I finally answered, realizing how ironic it was that I was able to
say the words now. "For some reason, I felt the need to explain
God's actions."

"That's not your job . . . but you know that," he answered.

"I know," I agreed.

"Your job is to be Jesus to them. God can handle His own defense."

I knew that my friend was right. Why had I felt the need to defend or explain God? Why couldn't I have been honest with the father and myself and say, "I don't know. But I do know that God loves us and God doesn't want us to hurt"?

Just like I did, Martha does what people of action do: She gives the "right" answer and prepares to move on. She gives the right answer, going so far as to affirm the orthodox Jewish belief in the life to come. And all the while, her real questions—her deep-in-the-soul questions—go unasked and thus unanswered.

Let me say this clearly: *God is not afraid of our expectations, doubts or questions.* I know I have said it before, but why do I, and maybe you, need to hear it so often? Because as the disciples lacked courage and Thomas lacked hope, Martha's reaction reminds us what happens when we lack *honesty* when we confront our spiritual struggles.

Despite her equivocation, Jesus replies to Martha with firm and clear words of hope. He announces that *He* is the resurrection and the life. What crazy words, uttered in the middle of a mourning period, standing at the door of a tomb! But He says them, and He intends that we hear them. Christians die physical deaths, but Jesus is talking about *real* life, the kind not burdened by pain and loss and grief.

But Martha misses it. She is so busy trying to make sense of the situation *for* Jesus that she misses His words of comfort for that day and every day to come.

Mary

When Mary hears that Jesus has arrived, she, like Martha, goes immediately to meet Him—and so do all the mourners. The scene is freighted with drama. As Mary approaches Jesus, the group of wailing persons surrounds them. It's not only distressing, but it's annoying as well.

As Mary reaches Jesus, the Scripture states that she kneels at Jesus' feet and cries, "If you had been here, my brother would not have died" (see John 11:32). She pours out her grief and confusion in a torrent of tears, unable to say anything else, and the Scriptures state that Jesus, witnessing Mary's reaction, as well as the reaction of the mourners, is "deeply moved in spirit and troubled" (v. 33). The *New King James Version* says that He "groaned in the spirit." We need to catch this: The Messiah *groans in agony* at the grief He is witnessing.

Jesus' response, which we will examine more closely, tells us a great deal about the depth of Mary's grief. This situation is so far removed from the day when she had sat at Jesus' feet to learn about the kingdom of God! Now she kneels at His feet, wondering why her world has collapsed. As we explored earlier, Jesus loves this family and has great affection for Mary. Her deep emotional distress moves Him beyond words.

Mary is overwhelmed and confused. She had heard Jesus teach about life and hope, but how can she believe in such things now? She is wounded. Her faith has been tested and feels as though it is broken. Of the four reactions, Mary's is the saddest and most spiritually wrenching. Unlike the disciples, Thomas or even Martha, Mary's mouth utters a few words but her heart remains silent, too distraught to voice anything. If anyone can see this heart silence, it is Jesus.

Mary's pain is the deepest kind. She's not angry or frustrated, for those feelings are the opposite of peace and understanding—which is at least *something*. No, she is, as a theologian friend puts it, simply *without*. The groans from within Mary are the sounds of a soul for whom God has disappeared. It is her emptiness that draws Jesus' groans in response.

The disciples resisted. Thomas courageously followed. Martha gave the right answers.

Mary simply gave up.

Standing at the Tomb

Tombs come in all shapes and sizes. How many times have you watched a person's life self-destruct while you wondered why that person couldn't understand, see the problem or make a different choice? How many times have we found ourselves a second too late or an inch too short to discover or take hold of something better? Do you live with any regrets? I do. Do you have any relationships you wish you could do over or take one more moment with? Certainly. Do you have any words or mistakes that you wish you could turn back the hand of time and make right? Who doesn't? Have you left anything undone because of doubt or fear or confusion that you wish you had one more chance to face? I bet we all do.

The four reactions explored above tell us much about the characters involved, but even more about ourselves. We see ourselves in these characters because death and mourning, of various kinds, are the great equalizers of humanity. Invariably, our true strengths and weaknesses emerge. Death knows no socioeconomic status, no nationality, no religion, no political persuasion, no good life or bad choices, no criminal or saint. The story of Lazarus is really the story of how we react when death and grief and trouble come a-knockin'; that is the reason for Jesus' tears.

Jesus didn't weep for Lazarus; he was in better shape than any of the others. Jesus wept for the mourners who were weeping without really knowing why. He wept for the disciples whose fears, once again, had gotten the best of them. He wept for Thomas, who had all the courage he needed but none of the hope he so desperately wanted. He wept for Martha, who could give the right answers but couldn't ask honest questions. And Jesus wept for Mary, who believed that God had vanished. But, friends, here is the beauty and burden of this passage: Jesus wept, too, for you and me, and for every lonely tomb before which we will ever stand.

You remember Carol, right? The crazy woman who turned out to be indispensable as both a volunteer in my new little church and as a friend? Well, for the next year, Carol arrived promptly at the office every Monday, Wednesday and Friday. She was a great help, not to mention a lot of fun. Behind the very ordered façade, I discovered a person who loved to laugh and enjoyed life. We shared a love for funny stories, and she would print out odd ones from the Internet and bring them to the office.

Our favorite was about a guy who arrived at the emergency room with an eggplant inserted in a very delicate part of his anatomy. When the doctor asked the gentleman how it had happened, he told the physician that while he was putting away his groceries, he had slipped and fallen on the eggplant. Carol and I remarked that this explanation made *perfect* sense, because we knew so many people who made it a habit to rush home from the market and strip completely naked to put away their groceries.

Sure, such jokes were irreverent, but irreverence was a part of our relationship. Carol and I became friends, and I realized that we served a purpose for each other: She provided great help and assistance, and I provided an outlet for a creative and talented woman who had almost decided that life had lost its luster. Looking back, those days in the makeshift office of that fledgling church were some of the happiest of my ministry.

Carol's health remained strong for a while, but doctors reminded her that her condition would not improve. The pancreas is incredibly important to the body's functions. It is a silent partner who says little but carries a very big stick—and we can't live without it. It helps to regulate blood sugar and energy levels, and plays an important role in fat dissolution. And when the pancreas is not working right, a person feels terrible and can experience great pain.

But Carol fought hard against the effects and arrived faithfully each week to volunteer. She continued this schedule for nearly a year, until one Monday she simply didn't show up.

Eventually, a diseased pancreas begins to work against the body's natural processes and goes into what one doctor friend describes as a "planned shutdown." The body does not know how to respond when this occurs, and most people experience acute and significant effects when it does. Carol was no exception; she awoke that Monday to excruciating pain, wrapped in nausea and malaise. She was admitted to the hospital, and by the time I arrived, Carol had been sedated.

Within days, Carol had undergone the first of several procedures that were performed over the next months to address one residual problem after another. Yet even though the pain was relieved with each attempt, the procedures left Carol weak. She experienced a slow decline from which she never fully recovered. One of the worst things about pancreatic disease of any kind is that it can take a long time for the worst of the effects to progress. Patients are left to cope day to day with simply not feeling well, battered by moments of what can only be referred to as acute agony.

One evening I arrived at Carol's home and found her husband and daughter very concerned. Carol had not gotten out of bed for several days and was now refusing to eat. Even worse, she had not taken her insulin, a necessity given the decline of her pancreas. Her husband met me at the door. "Shane," he said, "I think she has given up. I don't know what to do anymore. Can you talk to her?"

I went into her bedroom and found Carol lying in the fetal position. Gone was the strong, mischievous spirit. Instead, I discovered a frail, weak woman who had decided that this life was not worth living any longer.

"Carol," I said softly. She lifted her head and turned just enough to see me sitting on the edge of her bed.

"I see they called in reinforcements," she whispered.

"Everyone is very concerned about you," I replied.

"I'm fine," she said with The Tone. "I just need to sleep."

"Mike says you won't take your medicine or eat."

"He exaggerates. I've been eating. I just don't feel like eating what he is cooking."

"Well, this isn't Crescent City Grill," I said with a smile. Crescent City was Carol's favorite restaurant. She smiled back, knowing that I was making a point. "I know you don't feel good and that you are tired of this," I continued, "but you can't give up."

"And, why not?" she said. "My body seems to have given up on me."

"I didn't say you don't have a reason to *feel* like giving up," I responded. "You know I understand how tired you are. But you can't give up . . . *because of them.*"

Carol loved her family. She had a wonderful husband who took great care of her, and she was the mother to two daughters, one who was married and another, Leslie, who was just 10 years old. Carol and I had talked about how Leslie had never really known her mother to be completely well; Carol's sickness had started just months after Leslie was born. I understood how difficult this was—my daughters have never known their father apart from medicines or talk of health conditions. Although both of us believed our children were well adjusted and even seemed to have mature spirits because of our conditions, it seemed unfair to us both that any child, from such an early age, should encounter life constantly tinged with death.

But that was just one of the areas in which Carol and I understood each other. We both knew what it was like to get up and not feel good, to wonder if we would ever really feel well again and to think, some days, that it just wasn't worth it. Yet in our friendship, we encouraged each other, never allowing the other to venture too far down the road of self-pity.

"You need to eat and take your insulin," I said.

"All right," she said, clearly dejected. "The syringe is on the table. If you draw it up, I'll take it."

"How much do you take?" I asked. She told me an amount. I had never given anyone insulin and had no intention of starting now. Besides, Mike did this and always made sure Carol had the correct dosage. For some reason, though, I looked at the bottle; she had told me an amount that was six times what she normally took.

"Nice try," I said.

"I forgot you could read," she said with a smirk. It was the first time she had shown that usual Carol spirit. "I wasn't going to take it," she added. "I'm just tired."

By this time, Mike had walked into the room. I didn't think it would be helpful to share the "overdose attempt" with him, but I did let him know that Carol had agreed to take her medicine. I told him I'd make a food run while he got her meds ready. "What would you like to eat?" I asked Carol.

"A Big One from Ward's," she replied.

Ward's was a local restaurant that served the best hamburgers and chili cheese dogs. The Big One was a triple-decker, quarter-pound burger topped with cheese and chili. It was like death on a bun, but if Carol would eat it (and it didn't kill her), I would get her one.

"You bet," I replied. Mike left the room to get a syringe.

Carol whispered something. I couldn't hear her, so I leaned closer. "I can't do this forever," she said, fighting back tears.

"I know, and you won't—none of us will," I replied. "But while we endure, it does matter that we press on . . ." With that, I stroked her red hair and told her that I would be back soon with her burger. She seemed pleased as she closed her eyes.

We repeated this scenario several times over the next few months, until one day in a hospital room, Carol didn't have to do it anymore. She passed away with her family at her bedside.

I remember on the drive home thinking, *I hate death*. But as much as I hated death, I hated *dying* even more. There seemed to be something wrong, something so contrary to what the God I loved intended, in the way life can appear to be wasted as we transition from one place to another. And I hated dying because of what it does to those who remain after their loved ones are gone. With a world so wired together, dying seemed so out of place in the grand scheme of eternity.

As I drove, I realized that I was angry, but I wasn't sure at what. At first I was angry because of Carol dying, but it grew and became something more. I thought about how many times she wanted to be normal, to just have a day when she didn't have to worry about medicines or feeling bad. What she would have given to simply feel better—not just physically, but to feel certain, even for a few moments, that everything was worth it. I got angry for Carol and for me and for everyone else who gets up every day and refuses to give in, even when we secretly suspect that giving in might be easier.

Halfway home, I stopped at a mini-mart to get gas. As I waited to pay at the counter, I stood behind a young mother and her daughter. The child was maybe four years old, beautiful but disheveled. Her green eyes caught my blue ones, and we looked at each other and smiled. I remembered that Carol had green eyes, eyes that were finally shut and now resting—that they weren't filled with worry and pain and tears anymore. For a moment, the young girl made me feel better because with the loss of my friend, here stood a new opportunity for life. Maybe *this* green-eyed girl wouldn't experience sickness and heartache.

Just then, her mother jerked the little girl's arm and said, "Get up here, stop daydreaming." I noticed that the mother had placed a case of beer on the counter as she asked for cigarettes. "Colts with filters," she said. She said more to the little girl, and though the words weren't mean, her tone certainly was. I felt anger rising in me again, but it wasn't about Carol. Or at least not all about Carol. I stood looking at the little girl and her mother, realizing that this little one, too, was in the middle of a chronic illness, but it had nothing to do with her body, at least not yet. She lived with a chronic parent in a chronic world that didn't seem to get it or want it or even understand that they were dying without it.

What's the "it"? you ask. The "it" is hope and a future and real life. I was angry that while some were fighting to drain every bit from it before dying in a hospital bed, others were dragging their "inconvenient" children around to buy cigarettes and beer and missing the best opportunity for real joy standing right in front of them.

Walking back to my car, I counted in my soul all of the ways that this woman could do better and the reasons it seemed she never would—and why her little girl's life would be a sad by-product of neglect. She would likely grow up to repeat the same patterns and would miss the best things because she was consumed with the wrong things. (It felt like a long walk to the car.)

I undid the cap on my gas tank and began fueling. Parked on the other side of the pump was a huge, expensive SUV whose doors were open. Inside was a beautiful family. The father pumped gas while the mother arranged snacks and handed juice boxes back to each of her three children from a basket on her lap. The television was on, playing one of the latest children's movies, and all seemed right with the world.

Just then one of the children screamed, in a tone that would make my yellow lab puppy run up a tree, "*I told you I don't like grape!*" She apparently did not prefer the flavor of her juice box.

Her shriek was followed by a sibling's: "Mom, I told you I wanted the other chips!"

The mom patiently handed the second girl another bag of chips, returning the previous ones to the basket. The first sibling continued to scream.

The father looked up from fueling and barked (in what my wife calls a *not too nice* tone), "Give her the damn grape!"

The mother replied, "I'm doing the best I can!" The kid continued to scream. Like the mother in the store, the father said other words to his wife, words that were mean and hurtful because of how he said them. By this time, child number three chimed in because he wanted everyone to (in his words) "Shut up!" because his movie had started. All the while, the mother continued to hand out drinks and snacks while father pumped gas and fussed and the children screamed at her—and the world was not right! The mother looked over at me and smiled, but it wasn't a happy smile or even a courteous smile. It was the smile people give you when they would like to cry but can't.

By this time, the little girl and her mother from the store were on their way out. The mother was still dragging the child as they walked around the corner of the store, beer and cigarettes in hand. They had no car and my best guess is that they lived in the trailer park visible just over the hill.

I stood there pumping gas, wondering why it was taking so long, looking back and forth between the two scenes. On one side was a broken mother with a hurting child, and on the other were broken children with a hurting mother. I thought, *Why can't that child*, thinking of the little girl from the store, *be with that mom?*

I felt the impulse to stop the mom of the green-eyed girl and say, "Why don't you straighten up your act and realize what a blessing you have in that little hand holding yours? Put down that medicine in the bag and spend some time loving the best thing you will ever know. Because I know a mom who would have loved to have one more moment with her child, and she wouldn't have spent it hollering or fussing or finding a way to forget her own misery."

And then I wanted to turn on the SUV dad and kids: "And why don't *you* realize what a gift you have in someone who takes care of your every need and loves you and cares for you even though you act like little brats and don't appreciate anything she does? Because I know a child who would love to hold her mom again and not just to see what juice box or snack or video she could provide, but to really hold her and smell her and know that there is someone in the world who loves her best. And, sir, why don't you spend more time encouraging your wife and being thankful that she is healthy and here and that she cares about how your day is going and will make sure that your needs are met? Stop acting like she is your maid and your children's nanny. Why don't you treat her, instead, as the partner who makes your life meaningful? Because I know a husband who would give anything to hold his wife again and stroke her hair, even if it meant that *he* would have to spend every day taking care of *her*."

Just then, the pump stopped, and I realized that I had tears in my eyes and my hand gripped the gas nozzle and my teeth were clenched. I replaced the dispenser, took my receipt and got into my car. As I drove off, the lump in my throat began to hurt, but not as bad as the hole in my heart. I thought about Carol, about Mike, about their daughters. I also thought about my own family—when I had been good to them but also when I had failed and forgotten what really matters in this world. And I thought about those families, about that unappreciated mother and that green-eyed, thrown-away girl . . .

I stood at the tomb, and the hopelessness and disappointment and emptiness were too much. And so I wept.

That day at Lazarus's tomb, there were so many dead. Jesus stood in the midst of friends and strangers and followers and wondered why they couldn't see what He saw. *My disciples, you don't have to be afraid—I'm not. Thomas, you don't have to be a martyr—all you have to do is trust and follow and be amazed! Martha, don't you understand what I am saying? I'm not just fulfilling a religious objective—I'm talking about real life that lasts forever and makes this life look like a momentary displeasure. Mary . . . sweet Mary . . . don't give up— you sat at My feet for a reason. You knew that God was close that day. He is close now, even if you can't seem to find Him.*

Jesus stood there and looked from one to another, grieving all that death and wondering why it would continue to be so difficult for them and for us to see something better. Jesus wept for what they had done and had not done, for where they had been and for where they had refused to go. He wept for how the world had made them cynical, fearful, hopeless, confused and sad. The lump in His throat began to hurt and the hole in His heart began to throb, and it was too much . . .

He stood at the tomb, and the God of the universe wept. He wept because those He loved were living like they were already dead.

At the Tomb with Mary, Martha and Lazarus

Jesus dries His tears and tells those who are gathered to move the stone from the entrance to Lazarus's tomb. Martha protests, "He would stink by now!" (see John 11:39). What could Jesus possibly want in removing the stone? Maybe to see Lazarus one more time? But by now, the fourth day, his face would be so disfigured that even Jesus would not recognize His friend. Yet with a touch of frustration, perhaps, Jesus replies, "Didn't I tell you, Martha, that you would see the glory of God?" (see John 11:40).

They roll the stone away, and Jesus steps forward to pray.

His prayer tells us much about God's cure for chronic death. He begins by making it plain to whom He is talking, wanting those around to see the connection between themselves, this event and the Father. Then He calls Lazarus forth. A few seconds pass . . . and then Lazarus appears! The moment should have been heralded by trumpets and great fanfare, but instead Jesus simply says, "Unwrap him and let him go" (see John 11:44).

The scene is stark, simple yet powerful. It tells us how God works: He brings life where there was only death, and expects us to live like it.

In John 16:33, Jesus reminds His disciples, "In this world you will have trouble." I have often been struck by how true, but also how honest, a statement this is from God. In my life, I have known a lot of trouble. Hemophilia from birth, eye surgery, HIV and hepatitis-C, heart surgery—should I go on? I have also known the more personal, relational problems as well—broken friendships, betrayal, bad choices, the hurtful decisions of others. Yep, Jesus is right. In this world we have trouble. But if you think about it, it's pretty great of God to come out and admit it. He doesn't beat around the bush or paint flowery pictures— He's completely honest and straightforward: *Guys, while you are here, it may get pretty bad . . .*

And then He goes on: "But take heart, for I have overcome the world." Notice that Jesus doesn't say your troubles will get better or that your life will be easy. No, Jesus says to "take heart." I love that phrase. It comes from an ancient understanding of the relationship between parts of the body and different kinds of courage. Physical courage is found in the stomach, but the courage that causes someone to move through what seems to be a hopeless situation comes from the heart.

Through Jesus, God understands the troubles of this life and has made a way for us to "take heart" and begin to truly live. How did God do this? It goes something like this: God loved us and decided that we were worth dying for. God, in Jesus, came into the muck to become like us, not only to rectify the cosmic gulf between Him and us, but also to restore the brokenness in and between people. In doing so, God called us out of the tombs in which we sealed ourselves, unwrapped us from our doubt and sin and misery, and set us free.

But, friend, it is still up to us to come forth and be willing to be alive again. We have to stop living like those walking around dead, and start walking like a dead person who has been raised from the tomb. We must live like Lazarus.

6

The Sixth Encounter: Peter

JOHN 18:15-27; GENESIS 3; JOHN 21:1-23

*[The Church] should never consider it complete,
but must always be looking
to see who is missing, and doing everything
in its power to find them.*

SHANE STANFORD, *THE SEVEN NEXT WORDS OF CHRIST*

Have you ever been betrayed? I'm not asking if someone has hurt your feelings or said an unkind word. I don't mean, Have you been let down or wronged? No, I'm asking if someone you loved and who professed their love for you has ever willingly and methodically betrayed you. See the difference? Think about it for a moment.

We often loosely use the language of "betrayal," having been taught a particular meaning by the news media or reality TV. I remember the first time I watched MTV's *The Real World*. It was the beginning of the reality TV craze. Several people, who didn't know each other prior to the program, agreed to live together and have their every move and thought videotaped. Keep in mind that these folks did not have a say (or at least that's how it was billed) as to who they lived with. The results were both humorous and disturbing.

When you take folks who are willing to have their lives broadcast to the world, put them with other folks who want their lives broadcast to the world, and put them all in a house without giving them any clue as to each other's real identities, don't expect "the real world"—expect dysfunction. Add to the mix that it is their "job" to make television entertaining and interesting, even if it means exposing themselves (and, yes, I mean that in every way you can imagine) or selling out their roommates to get attention, and it becomes a great way to learn about narcissistic personality disorder.

Trouble is, in their efforts to turn "human drama" into a spectator sport, these shows do not portray the "real world." No, the human drama is far more delicate and subtle. Most people I know don't want their lives exposed for others to see. Quite the contrary; most folks in the "real world" keep secrets in hidden places. And they don't use the word "betrayal" lightly, because real betrayal is deeper than made-for-TV drama between strangers; it is nothing short of life-threatening and heart-stopping. I believe you know what I am talking about. When this kind of human drama is played out in our lives, we don't run to the corner and scream it to the world; we don't get in line to have our lives plastered on a television screen. No, when we betray or are betrayed, we stop in our tracks and wonder . . . we wonder how, amidst our rage and loss and shame, the sun could dare to come up on such a day.

The Trumpet Call (John 18:15-27)

Roman guards stationed in the city of Jerusalem divided the night into four *watches*, and at the end of the 3 A.M. to 6 A.M. watch, a trumpet sounded to indicate a change in the guard. The word describing this change, both from the Latin and Greek, means *cockcrow*. Which brings us to the human drama that unfolded between Jesus and Peter.

While sitting around the table for the Passover Meal, Jesus predicted that Peter would deny Him three times before the cockcrow. Peter was adamant that such a thing could not happen. Jesus simply looked at His friend, knowing the strength of words but weakness of action among His followers.

Of course, Peter was stronger than most. Reactionary, sure, but Peter never feared a challenge. He had been the only disciple to attempt to walk on the water (see Matt. 14:22-36), and lest we forget, while the other disciples were silent, Peter confessed Jesus as the Messiah (see Matt. 16:13-20). And yet, not too many steps into the sea, Peter began to sink, and not long after his glorious confession, Peter was rebuked by Jesus for misunderstanding His real mission.

Peter was brash, passionate and bold. And, although he had stumbled before, sitting around this table, he confidently proclaimed his unwavering support. Later, when the soldiers arrived with Judas to arrest Jesus, Peter grabbed a sword and defended his friend. Jesus stopped Peter's attack, but Peter had proven his point: He was a friend to the last.

Peter, maybe more than anyone else, represents the fragile nature of humanity, especially when the world becomes too real. After Jesus is arrested and taken to the high priest's home, the mounting anxiety takes hold. The other disciples flee, and though Peter follows Jesus, he lags far behind. He moves from shadow to shadow, staying close . . . but not *too* close.

Another disciple lets Peter into the courtyard of the high priest's palace. Here, Peter hears the discussion and wants more than anything to defend his friend. But for some reason, he is not as brave now. Time and the night have drained his courage, and he stands silent.

A maid is the first to recognize him. "Aren't you a follower of Jesus?" she asks. "I am not," Peter replies (see John 18:17). He moves quickly away.

A second time, a group of servants recognize Peter and ask if he is a follower of Jesus. Again, he denies it (see John 18:25).

Finally, another person asks, "Aren't you one of Jesus' followers?" Peter turns and, with a curse, denies his friend a third time (see John 18:26-27).

Just then, the trumpet for the guard change sounds the cockcrow. It is over. Jesus was right.

It's ironic. As Jesus is taken away, bound and beaten, accused of confessing that He is "I AM," Peter becomes all of us, hiding behind our fear, crying, "I am not."

Does Peter's behavior surprise you, or are you so familiar with this story that you've forgotten how to be shocked by such a stunning betrayal? Or perhaps Peter's treachery feels personal because you have had a Peter in your life who has betrayed you. I have.

Now, keep in mind that my life is an open book. Since the day I stood before a small church in southern Mississippi and asked them why they didn't want me to be their pastor, only to hear them respond, "Because you have HIV," I have allowed people into my life and thoughts. I have written about most of my interactions and feelings as an HIV-positive minister, sharing what it has been like to deal with the uncertainties such a condition creates. I have shared my journey before thousands of people. For years I have told my story, sometimes at the consternation of others, sometimes at their request, but I rarely hold anything back.

But I don't talk about betrayal much. As open as my life is in one sense, betrayal is just too personal in another.

The betrayal happened without my knowledge. Sure, I suspected that my friendship with this person possessed broken edges, and people had warned me about unhealthy patterns they had seen, but I tend to give people the benefit of the doubt. As it turned out, this worked against me.

The cock crowed on a Monday morning. The news of my betrayal was first revealed, and it was bad. The level of deception and duplicity went beyond anything I could have imagined. The details flowed in, running like venom mixed with tears. With one truth came another lie that led to more questions, followed by more confessions that pointed to more lies. Before it was over, the meaning of an entire five-year period of my life had been reduced to rubble. The friend, who, to his credit, had stopped the destructive patterns some time before the confession, had created a façade to protect his self-interests, and when the truth finally emerged, it became clear that no one else could know about it. The repercussions would have been too great. Leaked details would have affected not only my friend and me, but also our families and children. It was like a bomb had exploded, without anyone knowing the carnage it had caused.

Even with the shock and pain, I never thought of doing anything drastic, such as suicide or violence, though for the first time in my life, I could understand how someone might see such actions as solutions. I discovered that, when one has been betrayed, there is a need to *do something*, to find a way to make the pain stop. Oh, did I mention the pain? Even after growing up a hemophiliac with bleeding muscles and joints and taking medicines that make me feel horrible, I have never felt anything more painful than betrayal. There is no running from it, no sedation for it, no cure. It just hurts.

And then there was the rage. I am not an angry person by nature, but with betrayal, "by nature" is thrown out the window. We become, no matter who we are, "reactors," dangerously churning powerful, barely contained emotions on the inside.

Betrayal also brought self-doubt. *Where did I go wrong? What could I have done differently? Why did I trust him? What is wrong with me?* These were only the first questions. Before long, self-doubt became humiliation partnered with paranoia. *What if others find out? What if people knew what has happened? Would they be laughing at me? What about my family? What would they think?* Question after question, with scarcely a pause between them.

And then betrayal brought the worst of its plagues: hopelessness. *If he did this to me, what makes me think others aren't doing it or won't do it, too?* Before long, betrayal affects every corner of your life, including your spiritual core. After all, the roots of betrayal began there.

Betrayal in Paradise (Genesis 3)

Betrayal was born at the beginning, in the Garden of Eden, and it has infected us ever since. Picture it: Adam and Eve are having a grand time. They have their jobs (taking care of creation) and each other and, most importantly, they have God. I love the Scripture passage that says God was "walking in the garden in the cool of the day" (Gen. 3:8). What a scene! The Creator takes a stroll, looking for the pride of His creation. The feel of the passage is that God has walked here before with Adam and Eve and that He enjoys this time with them. Adam and Even don't see creation as work or a struggle; they experience God at His most personal, living as friends do. Things are perfect. The world is right.

But all too soon, the serpent spoke a beautiful, well-crafted lie, and Adam and Eve toyed with being their own gods. Oddly enough, I don't think they ever meant to hurt God. Most betrayals are not premeditated, but they are personal—and this was the first and most personal of all. Betrayal killed what held creation together. It was relational murder on a cosmic scale.

Adam and Eve, for the most basic and selfish of reasons, killed their relationship with God. They chose momentary pleasure—the thought of becoming their own rulers—over the long-term joy of knowing and walking in the cool of the day with the Creator. After the first bite of betrayal, Adam and Eve had only to look at themselves, ashamed by their nakedness for the first time, to realize what they had done. *What just happened*

here? You made me do it! No, it was your idea! And then Adam and
Eve did what murderers do. They fled, hid and crafted their al-
ibis, even though they knew there were none.

With this, the effects of the most grievous of betrayals took
hold in all of us. What seemed impossible perfection became
imperfect. Adam and Eve not only turned on God, they turned
on each other. Their souls became infected with the lie of self-
sufficiency, and they had no alternative but to believe it—and to
make more lies and, thus, more mistakes.

The scene shifts in Genesis 3:9-12 when God calls out,
"Where are you?"

Adam responds, "I heard you but I was afraid because I
was naked."

"Who told you that you were naked?" God asks.

"The woman *You* put here with me—she gave me some fruit
from the tree, and I ate it."

Then God says to the woman, "What is this you have done?"

"The *serpent* deceived me, and I ate," she says, in a classic
example of the blame game. Gone not only was the notion of
relationship, but also the truth and any sense of personal responsibility. But as bad as it was, that was not the worst of it.
There was more to come.

The passage says that Adam named Eve *after* the betrayal.
Before, they had not needed names because they really *knew*
one another. Betrayal broke not only the nature of relationship;
it dissolved its possibilities. Gone was the potential of one person living in real fellowship with another and enjoying the
blessing of the Creator. Now they hid behind their garments
and names, always aware that something stood between everyone—people and people, and people and God.

For you see, that was the worst damage of this first betrayal,
not that it broke these relationships (which was pretty damaging), but that it created in all of us a primal urge toward self-

preservation. After all, when betrayal enters the picture, who can you trust?

It's Catching

A friend of mine, who learned her husband had cheated on her, told me that she had never thought about having an affair until after she learned of her husband's infidelity. And, although she and her husband had decided to make it work and she desired for it to work, she admitted that she had recently had a sexual relationship with a married coworker. Their affair was brief, and they agreed it couldn't continue. But the damage had been done.

"Does your husband know?" I asked.

"No," she said. This surprised me.

"Well, if you didn't tell him about it, then why did you do it?" I responded.

"To get back at him," she said.

"But he doesn't know," I said, confused.

"But, now *I* have a secret," she replied. "And worse, when he suspected something, I lied to him."

Then she said it: "And that will hurt him most of all."

I could see where this was going, and it wasn't pretty. Here was my friend, a beautiful woman, on the inside and out, talking like a person possessed.

After her comment, we sat together in silence. It was an eerie quiet, much like what I expect the moments were like after Adam and Eve realized what they had done. The serpent had not told them what would happen next: *nothing.* They were no wiser; they weren't more powerful or more glorified. They just *were* . . . and strangely enough, they didn't know what to say or do. Not that they *couldn't* respond; it was worse than that. They didn't know *how* to respond. They had made a conscious decision to choose the serpent over the Creator. The serpent had promised a spectacular outcome, but Adam and Eve experienced . . . *nothing*. How do you answer, act or feel when you give away everything you know to be good and true, only to get nothing in return? I don't know either.

"Do you love your husband?" I said to my friend.

"Yes," she answered, her tone softer now.

I watched my friend for a moment and realized that I had seen the look on her face before. Not long before, my youngest daughter had brought me her favorite toy. It was broken, and she held it in her hands. Tears streamed down my daughter's cheeks, and she was unable to get the words out. But she didn't need words. The look said it all: *It's broken and I don't know what to do.*

Here my friend stood, not with the pieces of her favorite toy, but instead holding her broken heart. At that moment, she looked up at me, tears in her eyes, and I saw the same expression I had seen on my daughter's face: *It's broken and I don't know what to do.* I remembered fumbling for the right words before simply putting my arms around her and wondering how love could come to this.

My friend's reaction unnerved me, not just because it was out of character for her, but because I saw myself in it. Thinking of my own betrayal, I confessed that part of me had wanted revenge and retribution. And worse, I wanted the upper hand, the last laugh and the final plunge. *It is a vicious cycle,* I thought. *This is what Satan wanted from the beginning. It isn't just about wronging the one who wronged you; he wants us to re-create the lie and hurt enough that we eventually forget there is any other way.* And Satan's success has grown exponentially since then with every misstep.

Thinking of my friend's situation, I didn't have the heart to point out that she had become the enemy now, because the coworker she had slept with in order to get back at her husband was also married. He had a wife who loved him and thought that he loved her. Now my friend had become what she despised, all because her betrayal had convinced her that she could rectify her problems by perpetrating them on someone else. Satan had done more than trick her; he had made her "the other woman," the worst of what she scorned. And without her realizing it, the cycle continued and expanded.

But God knew exactly what would happen. That's why He tried to steer Adam and Eve away from choosing betrayal: "Don't eat of this tree. Don't take this first step, because once you do there is no going back. There is nothing on the other side of this fence but heartache and malice and rage and pain. I'm warning you, not because I am keeping something 'good' from you, but because I am protecting you. You can't handle this. You can't rationalize this. You can't manage this. *This will kill you*" (see Gen. 2:16-17).

It's been killing us ever since—killing us with vengeance when we are betrayed, and killing us with shame at our own treachery. And, friend, until a cross appeared on a hill and a stone was rolled away, that was the end of the story.

As the cockcrow sounds, Peter leaves the courtyard humiliated, dejected, angry, frustrated and ashamed. He leaves too human for his own skin, slipping away under the cover of darkness, much like Adam and Eve leaving the Garden. While his act of betrayal was unthinkable and his escape humiliating, it's the unbearable shame that hurts most.

This is our disease: We are afflicted by a lie that we too easily believe. As long as humans walk this earth—from Adam and Eve to Peter, from Peter to us—the cycle plays out: the *real* human drama in the *real* world, where people die from their secrets one guilty, painful, shameful breath at a time.

It's a Jungle Out There

One afternoon, I sat in the pickup line at our local elementary school waiting for my youngest daughter. The night before, my wife had read the previous section of this chapter—and had not liked it.

"You've got to lighten this up a bit," she said. "People know what you are talking about—I mean, we all sin and fall short and screw it up. But it's like taking all your medicine at once . . . it will just make you sick, and then what good is it?"

"But it's about sin and betrayal!" I countered, surprised by how strongly she felt about it. "We're not talking about daisies and pinwheels here."

"Look," she said, her eyes narrowing, "you wanted me to read the manuscript, and I'm telling you that it's a bit much for people to swallow at one time. That's what makes it so difficult to deal with . . . because we *know* it's sin and betrayal. It's not pretty and we don't like it. That's what makes people crawl back in the hole and think that God can't love them and won't forgive them. You can't leave the story hanging on this edge. Too many people may decide to jump."

And with that, she walked out of the room.

Well, that didn't go well, I thought. *Maybe I need to find a less dismal way to tell this story.*

The next day, as I waited for my youngest daughter to get out of school, my oldest daughter (who had been to a dentist's appointment) was in the backseat of our van. She was watching the movie *Madagascar,* the story of once-content animals from the New York City Zoo who decide they need to get a taste of the wild life. Marty the Zebra, helped by a group of militant penguins (looking to return to Antarctica) escapes to find that the "wild life" is not exactly like the brochure said. As is the case with most of us, Marty drags his friends (a lion, a hippo and a hypochondriac giraffe) with him until they find themselves out of the zoo and marooned on the island of . . . you got it, Madagascar.

For the first few minutes of the movie, I was sitting in the driver's seat just listening. But as the plot thickened, my ears perked up. Here is the short version: Marty is unhappy with his perfect surroundings. He believes things must be better on the outside. The penguins assure Marty that not only is life better on the outside, but they can help him get there. Marty escapes. Life is not better. He tries to make it right, but ends up taking his friends down with him. They blame each other and end up living in a place that is much less than paradise.

Does this sound familiar?

"Wait, I know this story," I said, not really talking to my daughter but needing to say it out loud. I climbed over the front seat and sat in the captain's chair next to her. *Now I can see what happens*, I thought. My daughter gave me a *not too nice* look, but she didn't ask any questions.

(I should probably stop here to mention that the pickup line at my youngest daughter's school is the worst experience one human being can survive. People begin lining up an hour early, which only guarantees that your car won't be hanging into highway traffic. It is a long wait. Long enough to watch *Madagascar*.)

Halfway through the movie, something happens on the island that no one is prepared for: The animals begin to act, well . . . like animals. The jungle does not bring out their best and, for the zebra and the lion in particular, their friendship—which seemed so natural in the comfortable confines of the zoo—now seems not only out of place, but at least for the zebra, a bit dangerous. After all, what does a lion in most other parts of the world eat for breakfast (or lunch or dinner)? You bet: zebra.

My favorite scene is when Marty (the zebra) and Alex (the lion) are together, scoping out the lay of the land, and all of a sudden, Alex bites Marty on the butt. Marty, who has never experienced this in their relationship before, turns and says, "You're biting my butt!" To which Alex replies, teeth still clenched around Marty's rump, "Naaaa I naaatt! (translation: "No I'm not!"). But obviously he is, and as you can imagine, this bothers

Marty. We can understand why. They had been friends, and now something is different. They feel separated, but they're not sure by what—and worse, they can't say why.

"*Aha!*" I shouted. "That's it!" My daughter turned and put her finger over her pursed lips, the universal sign for "Be quiet." But I didn't care! I had figured out a way to talk about our tendency to betray each other that wouldn't cause any readers to want to end it all! *Oh, man . . . I'll show Pokey!*

Like Marty the Zebra, our "wild life" instincts point us in directions we would never want to go, and we end up doing things that we would never want to do. But unlike Marty, we do these things not because our instincts are natural—we do them because our distant proximity to God is not.

The farther we get from our Creator, the less we know about Him and remember about Him. And yes, we even question whether He is real. We believed the lie and now we are abandoned. We have been told, maybe even too easily convinced, that things are greener on the other side, but once we find ourselves over the fence, we don't have anything and we are alone—and it doesn't feel good.

Alex had never bitten Marty's butt in the zoo—why is he doing it now? Because the longer they are away from their home, the farther they feel from each other. Alex increasingly forgets the importance of the boundaries that had been established for him, such as "Don't eat zebras." But once they are on their own, a new nature takes over—friends begin to feed on one another.

Of course, I was mumbling all this as the movie ended. My daughter looked at me and said, "Dad, you know this was just a movie, right?"

Her question offended me. "Of course," I said, as if it was no big deal that I had just made sense of the fall of humanity. "Please . . . what do you take me for?"

She turned back to the television and said, "A man trying to win an argument with Mom."

The Best Laid Plans

By now you're probably wondering what happened to this chapter and Jesus' encounter with Peter. To be quite honest, I am too. I had a perfectly devised outline: I would discuss the nature of sin and betrayal, its effects on the human condition, and then, how God puts the world back together one life at a time. And I'd use Peter as my prime example. It was going to be neat and profound, possibly even life changing! (Okay, maybe that's going a bit far.)

What happened? you ask. How did my life-changing sermon become my jumping over to the back seat of the van, mesmerized by talking animals, leaving my daughter to wonder why her father had lost his mind and was carrying on make-believe discussions with her mother? I'll tell you what happened. I was willingly distracted by a need to explain and validate my ideas about betrayal, because being distracted was easier than dealing with the scars of being betrayed. I was so angry in my own thoughts and feelings that my best intentions flew out the window.

What does this have to do with Peter? Well, I believe that Peter went to the high priest's courtyard the night of Jesus' betrayal with other intentions, too. I believe he went there for his friend and that he had every intention of helping Jesus. You don't go from cutting off a person's ear in defense of your friend to denying that same friend in one large leap.

No, Peter is caught off guard—he's not prepared to find himself standing at the door of the enemy's house having to make a decision, at first about his friend but ultimately about himself. What if he thinks for just a second that he can get away with the first lie, or that maybe he can even control it? Then he

might be able to help Jesus! And so, the first denial happens almost haphazardly. It isn't premeditated or even personal. The
first steps in betrayal usually aren't. After all, the serpent didn't
need to begin his conversation with Eve by asking if she would
like to screw up all of humanity. No, he simply hissed, "Did
God really say you couldn't eat of any fruit in the Garden?" (see
Gen. 3:1). And the game was on.

Later, Peter is standing around the campfire, feeling guilty for
what he has just done, but still determined to help his friend,
when he's asked the second time about his relationship with Jesus. He panics this time, and without much warning, he denies
Jesus again. *Oh, no*, he thinks. *What am I doing?* Peter is no longer
in control and the momentum is against him. He staggers from
the gathering, only to be confronted again. The Adversary doesn't
even need to lie to him any longer; Peter now believes the situation is hopeless. The Enemy only needs to place one more obsta-
cle in Peter's path: Another servant appears, asking the same
question of Peter, implying that he knows Jesus. One more denial, and just like that, the crock crows. It is finished.

What just happened here? Peter wonders as he flees from the
high priest's home in shame. *I came here for better reasons. This
isn't supposed to be how it turned out! How did it come to this?* I'll tell
you: one little flinch of the soul at a time, until Jesus' boldest
disciple ran like a coward from the scene, convinced that he had
gone too far to ever call Jesus "Friend" again.

Yet because of a place called Calvary, this was not the end of
Peter's story—and it's not the end of ours, either. But why is the
new chapter so difficult to write? Because, like it or not, the previous chapters of our lives mean something and have an effect
on us. They are not neat and easy. We can't help but replay the
past and relive the mistakes. No matter how we read them, we
can't walk away from the last chapters of our lives without understanding how ingrained the illness of the Adversary is in us.

It causes us to lie, cheat, hurt, deny and betray. It infects us at the most basic level, and once the disease grows, we lose our way, forget where we came from and end up living far, far away from our real home. As long as the Adversary can separate us from God and from each other, he can muddy the waters of God's grace enough that we are not sure if God can work in the midst of someone like us, even if there is a place called Calvary with a cross, and an empty tomb with the stone rolled away.

If we fail to acknowledge how deeply the previous chapters of our lives have scarred us, our "gospel" is too cheap. It is a gospel that does not understand the incredible magnitude of what Jesus did and does in and for us. He didn't just rectify a spiritual condition or pay a debt—no, He charged into the middle of a calamity that sought nothing less than to kill us.

So it is that Peter's Jesus-encounter sheds light on the rest of the encounters we have visited in this book. We feel utterly isolated, separated from God and others, because of too much—too much sin, too many mistakes, too much confusion, too much doubt, too much death—and we cheat our brothers and sisters (Zacchaeus), sell our bodies (woman caught in adultery), fear for our children's futures (man with the sick child), hate ourselves so that we despise everyone else (woman at the well), collapse under the burden of grief (Lazarus and friends), and yes, betray our best friends for no better reason than that we are afraid.

We're accustomed to lions eating zebras in this world because it's all that we have ever known.

Campfires and Questions (John 21:1-23)

Because we are so accustomed to this lions-eating-zebras world, the crucifixion of Jesus doesn't disturb us the way that it should. Most Christians envision a sanitized version of the Crucifixion—they have forgotten how truly gruesome it is. The one being crucified literally suffocates to death from the weight of his organs tearing in two. Finally, mercifully, the legs are broken and death is imminent. For those watching, the scene is unbearable. There is no honor in crucifixion. It is a criminal's death, a barbaric act reserved for the most reviled in society.

Thus, it must have been difficult to watch a man like Jesus be crucified, especially for those who loved Him most. They knew Him, and they knew His love for others. They had watched His compassionate ways and witnessed His miracles. He was no criminal.

But what could they do? The Romans were in charge—the authorities had decreed a death sentence. So Jesus was hung and died. By the end, only the women who loved Him remained. The men fled or watched from a distance. Crucifixion is not just about death; it is abandonment at the most personal level.

I can only imagine Peter's thoughts as he watched his friend die. I don't know if Peter remained on the scene or not. There is no record of his presence at the cross, but I can't help but think that he stayed—at a distance, sure, but close enough to watch. Maybe it is my fanciful opinion or my need to give everyone the benefit of the doubt, but I just can't believe that Peter, even after the denial, would have left his friend.

Of course, Peter knew things would never be the same. Jesus would die alone. Peter couldn't help Him, and he didn't have the courage to die with Him. Yet Peter's failure was in being too human, not in faking his love for Jesus. He wasn't brave anymore. He wasn't brash. But he also wasn't pretending when he professed his love for his friend. I believe Peter would have found a way to the scene.

He would have watched the moans and seen the agony. He would have seen the final breath. He would have witnessed Jesus' body being taken down, and he would have watched as they placed Him in a borrowed tomb. And I believe Peter would have turned away after the stone was rolled in place, wondering what would become of what was left of his soul.

The time following the Crucifixion was difficult. We often forget that before the glory of Sunday morning, Saturday dragged on in a nothingness that seemed as if it would never end. It wasn't the pain and agony of Friday. It was worse; it was *nothing*, like most "next days" are after a disaster.

Then on Sunday, Mary Magdalene announces that she had seen Jesus, and Peter and John race to the tomb. Scripture says that John outruns Peter. I've wondered if John really outruns him or if Peter hangs back, afraid of what he might find. I'm sure he has mixed emotions. No one wants Jesus to be alive more than Peter. But what if Jesus *is* alive? Certainly, He couldn't have forgotten what had happened at the high priest's house. The questions race in Peter's mind, punctuated with one phrase: *Jesus died alone.* Peter—first out of the boat, first to confess Jesus as Messiah—can never forgive himself for that. And he can't imagine that Jesus could, either. The horror of the Crucifixion was unspeakable, but the nails Peter drives into his own conscience are terrible, too.

To his amazement, Peter finds the tomb empty, and he returns to tell the disciples the news. Jesus appears to the disciples several times in the following days. Each time is magnificent, but even glory has limits when it comes to the human heart. With Jesus' resurrection, the real issue for Peter has little to do with stones rolled away or mystical appearances behind locked doors. No, one question remains: *Can one friend forgive another for doing the unforgivable?*

As is the case with most of us when tough times consume our lives, Peter returns to what he knows; he goes fishing. This may seem odd in the middle of the resurrection appearances, but for a fisherman who believes his relationship with Jesus is permanently changed (even in light of the Resurrection miracle), where else would Peter go? Several of the disciples join him.

The disciples fish without much success. That changes when a figure calls out from the shore, "Have you caught any fish?"

"No," they reply.

"Then cast your nets on the right side of the boat," the figure says (see John 21:6). Assuming it couldn't hurt, the disciples do what the man says.

The Scripture says that the catch is so great that the disciples can't haul the net into their boat. In fact, they drag the net full of fish to shore. But this story isn't about fishing. As the nets fill with fish, Peter's heart fills with something else—the familiar voice of One who he once knew well. John is the first to recognize Jesus: "It is the Lord!" he says (see John 21:7). Peter gets dressed, jumps from the boat and swims ashore.

Now this passage contains some important events that should not be missed, including the number of fish in the catch, why Peter was fishing naked and why the "right side" of the boat was significant. In truth, this is one of the most important passages for the Early Church, especially in relation to the mission of the first followers. (I discuss this passage in depth in another book, *The Seven Next Words of Christ*.)

But the heart of the story is Peter and Jesus. When Peter recognizes Jesus on the shore, he sees more than a familiar face. This is Peter's chance for redemption. Locked rooms, empty tombs and the previous encounters with Jesus after His resurrection meant wonderful things about the majesty of God's power, but they didn't answer the questions in Peter's heart.

This scene is different; it is personal. Peter had heard Jesus call from the shoreline before. This is *their* scene. In Luke 5, Jesus called the first disciples, Peter among them, while they were fishing. "Put out into deep water, and let down the nets for a catch," Jesus said (v. 4), and the rest was history. Today's calling, so reminiscent of that first day, is about redemption and restoration, and Peter knows it from the moment John calls out Jesus' name. Peter swims ashore and joins Jesus around the campfire—he knows his moment has arrived.

Jesus turns to Peter and asks, "Simon, son of John, do you truly love me more than these?" (see John 21:15). Scholars have debated what "these" are. Maybe He is referring to the other disciples, but I suspect He is pointing to the sea, the boats and the life of a fisherman. Peter had returned to what he knew best. We all do. But Jesus has other things, more wonderful things, in store for him. As much as Peter loves fishing, Jesus needs Peter to love Him more.

Peter answers, "Yes, Lord, You know I love You."

Jesus replies, "Then feed My lambs" (see John 21:15).

It may seem odd that Jesus would ask a fisherman to become a shepherd, but this is a new life and a new start for Peter.

Jesus asks the question two more times, and Peter answers yes to both. The third time, the Scripture says that Peter is grieved by Jesus' question, or at least by how many times He has asked. How many times had Peter denied Jesus? Right . . . three. This is more than an inquisition—the questions represent a reunion. The number three symbolizes completeness, but completeness often comes with discomfort and a price.

Peter's threefold denial had seemed an insurmountable and complete dissolution of his relationship with God. But a threefold declaration of love gives Peter the chance to answer again, and this time he is ready. Peter's denials had been about holding on to old patterns and answers; his answers now are the chance to do it over and get it right this time.

Jesus meets Peter on the shore of the sea and on the shoreline of Peter's life, and He restores him in a way that Peter will recognize forever. Jesus uses more than words; He uses the art of moving on and beginning again. In giving Peter the task of loving the sheep, Peter will always remember Jesus' love for him.

The first time Jesus had called Peter from the sea, Peter followed into the unknown. This time, Peter follows as one completely known and completely restored.

Confessions

Several days after I wrote the last paragraph of this encounter, I sent the manuscript to a friend for review. He finished it within the week, and we met at a local restaurant to discuss his suggestions. He had read over manuscripts before, and I was prepared for a list of grammatical edits and content shifts. However, I was not prepared for how this conversation would go.

We sat and placed our order. When the server left the table, I asked my friend, "So, what do you think?"

He looked down. This was was not a good sign. I imagined all sorts of reasons why he didn't like the manuscript. *Maybe the language was too flowery or the writing too conversational. Or maybe the theology was not well explained or the stories off center?* My mind raced.

"I loved it," my friend said. "Until the end."

I sat back, half-relieved that my friend had enjoyed most of it, but concerned about his rather serious expression when he talked about the book's ending. Even when he said he "loved" the book, his worried expression didn't change.

"I'm glad you liked *most of it*," I said. "But what about the ending?"

"Well," he said, glancing down. "The last encounter bothered me."

"Bothered you?" I asked.

"You wrote for nearly two dozen pages about betrayal and sin and loss," my friend said. "But you only give a few pages to what Christ did for Peter. I kept reading the chapter thinking, *Something is missing.*"

In response, I gave my friend an academic answer about Jesus' reaching out to Peter and about how He restored Peter's ministry. My friend wasn't buying it, or at least his expression said he wasn't. Yet he listened patiently as I used all of the right words to describe what God had done for Peter through Jesus. I even remember taking a napkin and drawing a picture to illustrate my answer (my systematic theology professors would have been proud). It took several minutes to make my case, and it felt more like a defense than an answer.

Finally, my friend reached across the table and touched my forearm, stopping both the movement of my hands (I need them to talk) as well as the flood of my words. He looked me in the eyes for a minute without saying a word. I just looked back. Somewhere deep inside of me, I knew what he was about to say.

"That's a great answer to the question, Shane," he said. "Too bad you don't believe it."

I was hurting and my friend knew it. I dropped my head, trying to fight back the flow of emotion. I explained that I had spent days working on this chapter. The process was very difficult. I would start and stop, unable to finish a paragraph. Or I would start and complete a section, only to read back through it and wonder why it seemed so angry and different from the other encounters. I actually started this particular encounter early in the manuscript. But with each delay, it moved further to the end. I assumed I couldn't finish it because I had some kind of writer's block. But the cause went much deeper.

"This is about *the situation*, isn't it?" my friend asked. He knew about the betrayal in my life and how difficult the pain of that relationship had been for me. He also knew that I had struggled to make sense of why it had happened. I blamed everyone, including myself. But, the more I blamed, the less I understood and the worse I felt.

"Yes," I answered. It was rare for me to answer with only one word, but I was having trouble saying anything at that point.

"You know it's okay to be confused," my friend said. I looked up at him. He had been a true friend for many years. He was also wise and insightful, and I trusted his counsel and intentions thoroughly. He knew I didn't like confusion. But there was a hesitation in me, even with him, to talk about the betrayal, partly because speaking of it at all made me sad and angry. There were edges to the story that I didn't understand, even about my own failings and blame in the situation, and it all seemed too complicated.

Whenever I am trying not to be emotional, a painful lump develops in my throat. I have always assumed that was God's way of not letting me hold things inside too long. It certainly wasn't helping now. Finally, I said, "I can't seem to make sense of this encounter."

"Maybe you're not supposed to make sense of it," my friend said. "Maybe you're just supposed to write what you feel. Most people reading this book are where you've been. They know about pain and betrayal all too well."

I looked at my friend and said, "Then what are we looking for?"

"Well," he said, "I don't know what everyone is looking for, but I know what people are *not* after. They don't need another academic answer. They know they hurt. They know things need to be better. And they know, deep down, that what they are trying isn't working." My friend waited a moment and then finished, "They know they need hope."

Hope. It seemed like a simple word, but I knew it was the line in the sand for why some of us make it and some of us don't. At that moment, it hit me: I had been trying to give an answer to a question that wasn't being asked. Peter, like the rest of us, doesn't want to know *why;* he needs to know, *Can this be put back together?*

That's why Jesus shows up on the shoreline, to give Peter hope—hope that the cycle would not continue and that things would be restored and made new. Jesus gives Peter hope that hearts do heal and lives do get put back together, if we will only trust the God who still walks on the water, moves stones away and meets His friends on the banks of their troubled lives.

Of course, I knew these things about Jesus. I had studied His life and loved Him for as long as I could remember. But I also knew that Jesus can't work with something a person refuses to give over to Him. I knew, sitting with my friend in that restaurant, that *you can't write about real hope unless you believe it for yourself.*

"This isn't about finding the right words, Shane," my friend said.

"I know," I answered. "But that would be easier."

He smiled and replied. "Yes, I guess it would. Shane, you've been through so much in your life. Don't live regretting what could have been. That's like living each day with a footnote at the bottom that tells about how good God is, except in the things we can't let go of . . ." My friend paused. "You deserve better than footnotes."

My friend didn't need to say anything else. I knew what he meant and what needed to happen. I had been doing this a long time. It wasn't that God had not been working in me about my feelings. It was that I didn't want to listen; I'd decided that I could get by, maybe even fake my answers by using all the right words. But that's not what God expected, and it's not what I needed.

As I got up to leave, I thanked my friend for both his patience and his guidance. He put his arm around my shoulder and placed a folded piece of paper in my hand. "Read this," he said. "It's as easy as 1-2-3." I laughed, wondering what he meant.

After getting to my car, I opened it and found these words: "I lift my eyes to you, O God . . . Have mercy on us . . . for we have had our fill of contempt" (*NLT*). At the bottom of the paper was the reference. The words came from Psalm 123. *As easy as 1-2-3* . . .

This was my prayer that day. I was tired of being angry. I was tired of wondering why. I was tired of feeling betrayed. And, in response, I was tired of being unforgiving and hypocritical. Mostly, I was tired of Satan's control over this part of me. I had experienced my fill of contempt. I wanted something better for my life. God did, too.

On the Shore with Peter

I stood outside an office building for nearly an hour—I didn't know what time the person I had come to see would leave work. I had not called. Maybe I thought he would not answer my call. So, when I saw a car I recognized in the parking lot, I took a chance and pulled in to wait.

After I had stood there for a while, it hit me that someone who didn't know me but somehow knew the circumstances with this person might worry about me waiting outside. In retrospect, it looked kind of ominous. But what can I say? I didn't have much history in confrontation, so my style was a bit rusty. I didn't even know what I would say; after all, this was a broken relationship, torn at the deepest level, the level where people trust one another. Yet I knew this was the right thing, even if I didn't have all of my questions answered. I knew I couldn't be healed or become a healer for others if I didn't face this situation. This was my shoreline, and Jesus was calling me to the campfire for a talk.

The person came out the front door of the office building and saw me standing by his car. He hesitated, but then made his way toward me. I stepped into his path.

"What do you want?" he said. He seemed angry.

My first reaction was not good. *Why is he angry at me? He is the one who threw away a life-long friendship.* I could feel the frustration building. The Adversary wouldn't let this go without a fight.

"I think we need to talk," I said.

"There really isn't anything left to say," he replied. "I made a terrible mistake and you made your decision, Shane."

"My decision?" I said, feeling a bit defensive.

"Yes, your decision." He responded. "You decided the grace and forgiveness you've always talked about did have boundaries and limits. And you decided that I had crossed that line and there was no going back."

I stood there feeling very human. I wanted to respond in anger, to build my defense, to talk about how *I* had been wronged. I wanted to shake him and scream, *"Why did you do it?"* The emotions raged. I slipped my hands in my pockets, ready to turn around and forget about trying to make it better. But my hand touched the paper my friend at the restaurant had given me, and I remembered . . . *I am tired of contempt.* It had killed my friendship, and now it was killing me. I realized the Adversary wanted this. He needed to keep the wound open. As long as it remained unhealed, the infection burned. I was tired of this. I was ready to heal my wound.

I took my hands out of my pockets and relaxed my arms to my side. I backed away from my friend, turned to the side and leaned against the car. My head was down. "You're right," I said. As the words came, it was as if my soul exhaled.

"What?" my friend asked.

"You're right," I responded. "I preached one thing, but when this all went down between us, I decided that it was too much even for God to handle."

My friend stood there, and then he dropped his head. He put his briefcase on the hood of the car, turned and leaned against the car, too.

"I didn't mean to screw it all up," he said. "You were a good friend." He looked into the air, and then back to the ground.

"At first, I thought I could handle things, and no one would get hurt. After I realized things were spinning out of control, the lies were too big to manage. Before long, I couldn't tell right from wrong, and I knew I had crossed too many lines to come clean."

"But you did come clean," I said, "and in good faith you came to me for help. I let my anger and disappointment get the best of me, and I forgot the first rule of the gospel—we treat others the way Christ has treated us." I paused a moment.

I took a deep breath and then looked at my friend. The next words were difficult. "I betrayed you in a much worse way," I said.

My friend narrowed his eyes and said, "What? How?"

"Sure, you betrayed our relationship, but then you realized that God expected other things, better things," I said. "You came to me believing that even in something like this that God could work." I waited for a moment before saying the next phrase. "But I betrayed you when I decided that no matter how much God expected from us, even in something like this, I didn't care."

My friend closed his eyes. Tears filled the edges.

I began again. "But I do care. I care for you and for me. I care that grace and forgiveness are big enough for this situation. And I care that God can work even in something like this. I guess I'm tired of feeling everything other than what God intends for us. And . . ." I put my hand on my friend's shoulder. "I'm tired of living life like there's a footnote at the bottom of each day's page."

My friend looked at me.

"I'll explain later," I said.

We stood there for a moment.

"I'm sorry," he said. "I really didn't mean for this to happen. If I could take it back, I would . . . but I know I can't."

"None of us can," I said. "That's why God tells us to move on. We waste too much precious time trying to fix things. God says, *Why not just forgive and get on to something better?*"

"I like that plan," my friend said.

"Me, too," I replied. "How about some coffee?"

"You buying?" my friend asked with a smile.

"Please . . ." I said. "I've been standing out here for an hour. Half your coworkers think I'm a stalker. The least you can do is spring for the coffee."

We laughed.

"You've got a deal," he said.

Peter went on to do more than make things right. He fed the sheep and loved the lambs. To his end, Peter confessed that not only did he know Jesus, he also loved Him and would die for Him. According to ancient sources, Peter bravely preached the Good News of Jesus from Jerusalem to Antioch to Rome. Eventually, near the end of Nero's reign, Peter—the one who once denied Jesus and then watched Him die on a cross—was crucified himself, except that he asked to be hung upside down out of respect for his friend. No one questioned Peter's loyalty or his courage ever again.

My friend and I continue to rebuild our friendship. We are stubborn and oftentimes much too human, but God is gracious and forgiving to both of us.

What about you? Did this encounter make you wince? Did you see your own betrayal, your own broken edges? Maybe you didn't even finish it, but jumped to the last page (I do that sometimes, too). Heck, maybe you went and rented *Madagascar* and considered the conversation done. Or maybe, just maybe, you thought about your own lost Gardens and about the footnotes in your life, and you decided to meet Jesus at the shoreline for a campfire talk. And then maybe, like me, you got tired of being filled with contempt, craved something better and decided to do something about it.

I hope you did.

I hope you did because God has more for us than the lies we have too often believed from the beginning. God still calls to us in the cool of the day, "Where are you?"

And through Jesus, we now answer, "Right here, Lord."

No more lies; no more hiding. This is the real end of the story, because it is not the end of us. What a beautiful day.

Finding God

Becoming a Christian might look more like
falling in love than baking cookies.
DONALD MILLER, SEARCHING FOR GOD KNOWS WHAT

I write to resolve questions and problems that I wonder and worry about . . . and that I know other folks are concerned about, too. I go to the life of Christ for answers because He is real and genuine and available. He teaches me about living and about why life has purpose that is deeper than buying things and becoming things. Jesus is more than a far-off God to me. He is my Guide, Counselor and Friend.

The gospel reminds us that we have been created for better. I believe that we were built for relationship and wholeness with God as well as with each other. The gospel also reminds us that what we experience in this world often is not the abundant life God has in store. But I probably don't need to convince you of that. To paraphrase C. S. Lewis's words in *Mere Christianity*, there are too many crooked lines out there for us to forget that somewhere there must be a straight line. Crooked isn't crooked unless there is straight.

Friend, Jesus confronts our crookedness because He knows straight. Yes, He knows our fears, our limitations, our accusers, our questions and our grief—but He also knows our future. We belong to Him and He will not let go.

I hope that as you've read this book, you have caught a glimpse of how Jesus reaches even into the darkest parts of our souls to find us. He hasn't gone anywhere. He certainly hasn't disappeared. Actually, *we* have been hiding—hiding from God, from each other and even from ourselves.

The folks in these encounters were hiding too, and now they want to believe and belong again—but they, too, feel too far gone. From Zacchaeus to the woman caught in adultery to Peter, the consistent thread is that God shows up and offers a way back to what was intended, a glimpse of how it should have been and—best of all—the hope that they can still have abundant life.

Finding God is not always easy, but not because God has gone anywhere. No, it is difficult because we forget where to look, or we forget why we care or that it even matters.

But God keeps showing up.

We Christians often make things complicated and take ourselves way too seriously. We convince ourselves that how good we are (or aren't) is the key to whether or not the "Jesus formula" prospers in us. We too often believe that our church pedigree (or lack thereof) defines the depth of our faith, and we're eager to buy the lie that one misstep or broken edge and God just won't be able to love us anymore.

But God keeps showing up.

He is tenacious, undaunted and very much in love with you and me. He showed up first in the life of Jesus and now He shows up through the lives of His people. Far from having disappeared, God is much closer than we imagine.

But sometimes, in the midst of a struggle, we find it hard to remember. Such was the case with me when I had heart surgery. One person who saw how lost and lonely I felt and whose support meant a great deal to my family was our next-door neighbor Chris. Every day from the time we entered the hospital, Chris sent a Bible verse and a "devotional theme for the day" via text message. It never ceased to amaze me how perfectly each day's Scripture passage fit the particular issue we faced.

The day I was to take my first walk around the hospital, the verse came from Isaiah, reminding me that I would mount up like wings of eagles and "walk and not be faint" (Isa. 40:31).

The third day after surgery, when all surgery patients face that mystical but all-too-real "wall of pain," the verse encouraged me to "be strong and courageous" (Josh. 1:9).

The day I woke up feeling particularly concerned about what would happen next, the verse echoed Jeremiah's words of a God who "knows the plans He has for us . . . plans for good" (see 29:11).

God kept showing up.

Every day was a new day—not always easy, but wrapped in the sweetness of God's Word sent sincerely and humbly by one of God's most precious servants. I could not have had a better pastor during those difficult weeks. Chris is not an ordained or professional preacher. He works at a church, but doesn't have the title "minister." His love, support and encouragement through an incredibly dark time reminds me that the best of who we are in Christ has little to do with titles or training, and everything to do with our hearts and proximity to Christ. Any one of us, lay or clergy, can learn a thing or too from Chris about being Jesus to those around us.

My next-door neighbor stands as proof that I don't need to look far to find God. In fact, when I need to see Him, I just step out on my front porch and look to my left.

We are not alone. God has not disappeared.

ᘉ Study and ᘙ Reflection Guide

*Living by grace inspires a growing consciousness
that I am what I am in the sight of Jesus and nothing more.*

BRENNAN MANNING, *THE RAGAMUFFIN GOSPEL*[1]

The following Study and Reflection Guide is designed to help you dig deeper into the lessons of the six encounters and apply what you discover to your spiritual journey. You can move through the book and Study Guide on your own, with a partner or with a group.

Each section below is designed to help you explore one of the encounters for one week. Begin by re-reading the primary Bible passage for that week's encounter. Then spend some time studying one of the *Discover* passages; there is one for each day of the week. The *Deepen* questions then serve as your opportunity to reflect on the primary principles of each encounter and apply those principles in your relationships with God and others.

Do this throughout the week, allowing your thoughts to percolate and evolve as you study God's Word and connect with Him in prayer. The suggested *Prayer Focus* in each section offers a beginning for your conversations with God; you may end up in a very different place as God reveals who you are, to Whom you belong and who around you is in need.

There is no right or wrong when working through these reflections. Just be sure to listen for Jesus' voice. As you do, He will help you find the God who has already found you.

Introduction:
Living in *Miseri* . . . Abiding in Possibility

Discover: Colossians 2:6-10; Philippians 2:5-11; James 1:19-27; 1 Thessalonians 5:14-22; 1 Corinthians 15:58; Matthew 5:13-16; Acts 2:42-47

Deepen: Many of us have felt the same hopelessness and fear as the people who met Jesus in the six encounters. *Can God forgive my past? Will Christ accept my meager pleas? Is it possible for God to love me even when I doubt or feel unsure? Does God even care?* Whether you believe it or not in this moment, we serve a God who loves us passionately and who is neither afraid of our mistakes nor repelled by our fears. Consider for a moment the potential of God's love for you and of a life restored.

1. What are the broken places in your life that keep you living in misery? Make a list of your broken places, whether dreams, mistakes or relationships.

2. What keeps those broken places from being restored?

3. What "first steps" do you need to undertake in order to heal?

4. Why is it important for the Church to live life together as a means for helping one another heal the broken places of our lives?

Prayer Focus: Those who feel too far from God.

The First Encounter: Zacchaeus

LUKE 19:1-10

Discover: Romans 8:29; Colossians 1:15; 1 Corinthians 4:7; Psalm 71:5; Micah 6:8; James 4:8; Joshua 1:9

Deepen: The story of Zacchaeus is familiar, possibly too familiar. Many times, we focus on the children's version with the "wee little man in a tree," and we miss Zacchaeus's heart-wrenching search for peace with God and his neighbors. This encounter highlights both personal responsibility and God's faithfulness to accept and respond to our lives wherever He might find us. As we navigate through our own spiritual crowd of pre-conceived ideas to join a real man in a tree, Zacchaeus's feelings of rejection, shame and guilt are all too familiar.

1. The Bible says, "Come near to God and he will come near to you" (Jas. 4:8). God promises to come close, even though He knows the "garbage" in our lives! Make a list of the trash that needs to be packed up in your life and taken to the street. How does your garbage keep you from seeking God in your life?

2. What are you willing to do in order to catch a glimpse of Jesus? What keeps you from acting on it?

3. In what ways can you respond to God today in order to make right your broken relationships with Him and with others?

Prayer Focus: Those looking to repair broken relationships.

The Second Encounter:
The Woman at the Well

JOHN 4:1-42

Discover: Romans 12:1-2; Proverbs 16:4; 2 Corinthians 3:18; Hebrews 13:2; Matthew 25:37-40; Titus 3:5; Philippians 3:12-14

Deepen: Inward shame breeds outward attitude, or at least it did for the woman at the well. In this encounter, Jesus confronted human need at its deepest soul-tearing level, and the woman, an outcast from her own people, discovered her faith in Jesus' discovery of her. She also realized that removing the barrier between "good religion" and real faith begins with a recognition that there are some needs no worldly relationship can meet. Jesus quenched a thirst the woman was afraid to admit she had. The woman exposed the dry, cracked places of fear, guilt and doubt that gnawed within her and drank from a grace that promised to never leave her thirsty again.

1. The Bible says to present ourselves as "holy and living sacrifices" (Rom. 12:1), but we contaminate our lives with bitterness, bad decisions and wasted opportunities. List those areas of bitterness or regret that keep you from seeing God in your daily life. What keeps those places so raw and unhealed?

2. Reflect on the story of the Two Marys (one actually named Harriett). What made their lives so different? What did they have in common? How are we all similar?

3. Do you celebrate God's knowing everything about you? Why or why not?

4. Jesus purifies our lives with grace, restoration and hope. Name your blessings (one by one, if you can) through which God speaks to the deepest places of your soul and gives you hope.

Prayer Focus: Those searching for acceptance and affirmation.

The Third Encounter:
The Man with a Demon-Possessed Son

MARK 9:14-29

Discover: Romans 8:28; Hebrews 4:16; Psalm 27:14; 1 Corinthians 1:30; 2 Corinthians 12:8-10; 1 Peter 4:12-13

Deepen: What is your greatest fear? If you are a parent, like the father in this encounter, what about the thought of helplessly watching as your sick child fights for life? His story touches the fragile, vulnerable places of human existence. Jesus met a father who wanted to believe, but because of circumstances, didn't know how. This passage is about limitations—the boy's struggle with the demon, the father's struggle with unbelief and the disciples' struggle to heal them both. God understands our limitations and desires that we not remain bound by them.

1. Why does Jesus' frustration both teach and comfort us as to how much God loves and accepts us?

2. The Bible says to "wait patiently for the Lord" (Ps. 27:14). But that is very difficult, especially in hard times. Life's limitations create three kinds of unbelief—those who *can't* believe; those who *won't* believe;

and those who *want to* believe, but don't know how. Which one are you? Why?

3. Make a list of things for which God can't forgive you. It's a short list, right? If God's love knows no limits, then neither must our limits define how we connect to God.

4. Thinking of Matthew, the little boy with AIDS, why is it important for us to live faithfully as the Body of Christ in the world? What difference does it make to be the "hands and feet" of Jesus to the most vulnerable among us?

Prayer Focus: Those dealing with the illness of a loved one.

The Fourth Encounter:
The Woman Caught in Adultery

JOHN 8:1-11

Discover: Romans 8:38-39; Matthew 9:11-12; Romans 15:7; 1 Corinthians 5:17; Psalm 72:12-14; 2 Chronicles 7:14; 1 John 1:9

Deepen: Many of us believe that we know this story, but do we? As the woman landed at Jesus' feet, the scene collides with our hearts and minds, unfolding from many angles. Jesus seemed to know the road that led her to His feet and the condemnation that had so defined her; He knew the woman. But He also understood that adultery doesn't happen alone. Make no mistake: As the woman lay abandoned in the dirt, Jesus knew her accomplice. Finally, Jesus knew that the woman's accusers had all, in their own way, committed adultery against God. And isn't that the case with us all? Stoning another person means not having to focus on our own sins. Jesus saw the inner workings of the human heart. We cannot leave this scene without a keen sense of God's seriousness about the problem of sin in each of us as well as the power of forgiveness for all of us.

1. Sin is a sickness from which all of us suffer. Why is the darkness in our lives so difficult to recognize and oftentimes so hard to confront?

2. What keeps you "landing at Jesus' feet" in need of forgiveness? Who accuses you today? Or are you another character in the story? Are you the accuser of another brother or sister? Are you the accomplice?

3. Reflecting on my friend Sophie's life, why do we rush to judgment when perceiving others? How does our sin in not accepting others with the grace of Christ continue the cycle of sin and brokenness?

4. The Bible says that "nothing can separate us from the love of God" (Rom. 8:38). God's grace heals our hearts and then moves us forward. Jesus says to go and sin no more. Is that possible? Why or why not? What might "sinning no more" look like? What keeps that picture from becoming reality in your life?

Prayer Focus: Those needing to repent and be restored from damaging life choices.

The Fifth Encounter:
Mary, Martha and Lazarus

JOHN 11:1-44

Discover: 2 Thessalonians 2:16-17; Psalm 147:3; 1 Peter 5:7; Isaiah 41:10; Deuteronomy 31:7-8; Revelation 21:4; 2 Corinthians 7:10

Deepen: John 11 runs deeper than the miracle it describes. The encounter begins with the confusion and misunderstanding of the disciples. Then Thomas speaks up with plenty of courage, but missing genuine hope. Next we find Martha lamenting to Jesus, "If you had only been here." She says the right words, but she doesn't share her honest feelings. Mary arrives wanting to believe, though the grief is too great even for words. And finally, of course, we have Lazarus, still in the tomb, the involuntary center of the drama. By the end, we see hearts and faiths struggling to understand Jesus' proclamation that life and death belong in God's hands. Jesus raises Lazarus and entreats some bystanders to free him from his burial cloths; after all, why should living folks live like dead ones? The four different reactions to Jesus and the situation leave us to wonder who the "dead ones" in the story really are.

1. The Bible says to "give our worries and cares to God because He cares for you" (1 Pet. 5:7). God grieves to watch His children live as those who don't know the real source of life. Which character are you in the story? What keeps you from seeing God's hand working at the tombs of your life? In what ways do you need to be honest with God?

2. Reflecting on my assistant Carol's story, why does a crisis make us stop and cherish people, places and

moments more? Think of those moments you wish you could revisit in your life. Why? What are some ways you can treasure what is most important to you before the crisis comes?

3. To whom do you need to reconnect today? What has kept those relationships broken or strained?

Prayer Focus: Those who grieve and those who are filled with fear and hopelessness.

The Sixth Encounter:
Peter

JOHN 21:1-23

Discover: Ephesians 4:32; Isaiah 1:18; Romans 4:7; Matthew 5:44; Jeremiah 3:22; Colossians 1:21-23; Acts 8:22-23

Deepen: Calling from the shoreline, Jesus invited the disciples, who were fishing, to have breakfast. Peter jumped from the boat and swam ashore. The chapter describes Jesus and the disciples sitting around the campfire as Jesus began to question Peter's love for Him. The scene not only marks Peter's redemption; it unveils the key to his restoration: Christ knew Peter's future, and He wanted Peter to understand it as well. Just days before, Peter's ministry, not to mention his life, was in shambles, but Jesus not only forgave Peter, He offered him a chance to change the world—not with swords or rebellion, but through love and service. No one's past or present prevents God's love calling them into their future.

1. The Bible says that through Christ, God has brought us back to Him as friends (see Col. 1:22). When the going gets rough, human nature returns us to those things we know best. Thus, the disciples went fishing, so Jesus met them on the shore. Where are the shorelines of your life from which Jesus calls for you, His friend, to return home?

2. The animated movie *Madagascar* suggests that lions eat zebras because that is all they have ever known. Why is the lie of self-sufficiency, told by Satan from the beginning, so easy to believe?

3. Think about the nature of betrayal in your life. Why does betrayal hurt so much? Are there those who have betrayed you? Have you betrayed someone? Describe your emotions and what has prevented you from reconciling.

4. The Bible says that "since God loved us that much, we surely ought to love each other" (1 John 4:11). We are to love and forgive one another. Make a list of those whom you need to forgive. Make a list of those from whom you need forgiveness. What keeps you from taking the next steps toward reconciliation?

Prayer Focus: Those caught in the snare of betrayal.

Note
1. Brennan Manning, *The Ragamuffin Gospel* (Sisters, OR: Multnomah, 2005).

Engaging the Silence of Unanswered Prayer

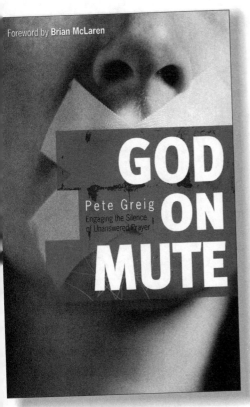

Foreword by **Brian McLaren**

GOD ON MUTE

Pete Greig
Engaging the Silence of Unanswered Prayer

God on Mute
978.08307.43247

Pete Greig, the acclaimed author of *Red Moon Rising*, has written his most intensely personal and honest account yet in *God on Mute*, a book born out of his wife, Samie's, fight for her life and diagnosis of a debilitating brain tumor. Greig asks the timeless questions of what it means to suffer and pray through the silence because your prayers seem unanswered. It is this silence, Greig relates, that is the hardest—the world collapses, and then all goes quiet. Words can't explain, don't fit, won't work. People avoid you and don't know what to say. So you turn to God and you pray. You need Him more than ever before. But somehow . . . even God Himself seems on mute. In this heart-searching, honest and deeply profound book, Pete Greig looks at the hard side of prayer, how to respond when there seem to be no answers and how to cope with those who seek to interpret our experience for us. *God on Mute* is a story of faith, hope and love beyond all understanding.